GOOD
CHILDREN

a common-sense guide
to bringing up your child

Lynette Burrows

FAMILY PUBLICATIONS

OXFORD

© Lynette Burrows, 2002

published by
Family Publications
6a King Street, Oxford OX2 6DF, UK
www.familypublications.co.uk

ISBN 1-871217-38-5

printed by
The Cromwell Press
Trowbridge, Wilts.

picture credits
Page 8, top: by courtesy of the *Daily Mail*
All other pictures were taken by family members,
and their copyright resides with the author.

front cover
Three grandchildren: Annie, John and Marie-Louise

back cover
Full House! Lynette, Ken and (grown-up) children:
front row (left to right) Matthew, Sophie, Claire, Oliver, Riffen.
back row (left to right) Mum, Ashley, Will, Emma, Alex and Dad.

Contents

Lynette Burrows

Preface to the third edition

You can never remember the way you were brought up. Childhood has its good times and its dramas but the idea that there was a method behind the way your parents brought you up, simply does not occur to most people until they are old enough to notice the differences between families. When you have your own family, of course, you begin to think seriously about how best to treat children in order to make both them and you happy and fulfilled.

This is the third edition of *Good Children*, which was first published in 1985. All six of my children were then at home and I had been writing notes for the book for years before it finally made it to the publisher. The idea was to pass on to other mothers the simple, practical, time-honoured ways of making child rearing less of a chore. So many childcare writers, then and now, are either men or professional women with very little hands-on experience of bringing up children, and the subject has been made to appear tremendously difficult.

I would be the first to agree that the job of child rearing *is* tremendously important and that, at times, it can be difficult. But then, there is no worthwhile job on earth about which you cannot say the same. Where I disagree with the so-called experts is that I say that most women have an instinct for the job and that, by taking advice from other women who have brought up children successfully, they can manage to do a perfectly adequate job themselves.

What has happened in recent years, I believe, is that professionals have actually got in the way of genuinely good child rearing. They have their mad, passing theories much as they have always had. Back in the 18th century, doctors believed in leaving nappies unchanged because the urine was good for an infant's skin! They also thought that giving them red wine with butter dissolved in it was good for their blood. By the 19th century they were happily referring to their discarded theories as old wives' tales, and had turned their attention to the subject of children's moral character instead. Great importance was then attached to flogging boys at school; and solitary confinement and bread-and-water diets for naughty children were much advocated by professionals.

The twentieth century was notable for two destructive theories that mirrored one another; the second of which is still, unhappily, with us. The first was that showing physical affection for your children made them into "moral invalids" later on. This theory, which held sway amongst professionals from the 1920s until the late 1950s, is now almost completely buried and no programme or expert ever refers to it. However, it was very influential in its day and was the reason, amongst other things, that children in hospital were not allowed visits from their mother – who might want to kiss and cuddle them. It is also the reason why foster parents were shunned in favour of institutions that would not spoil children by displays of physical affection, which could "seriously damage a child's chance of happiness".[1]

We now have a similarly amazing theory, about the physical correction of children, and precisely the same techniques mentioned above are now being used to discredit the practice of parental chastisement. Just as at one time affectionate parents were said to be unable to stop affection turning into incest, so parents today are supposed to be unable to tell the difference between a smack and a serious assault. Just as the anti-affection brigade used to refer to parents "fondling" their children, to give a negative interpretation of the cuddling of children, so now the same manipulative technique is being used to make parents think smacking is wrong, by calling it "hitting".

In this new edition of *Good Children*, there have been surprisingly few changes to the text. Footnotes have been added to draw attention to new facts which may be useful to today's mothers. For example, I wish I had known before how easy it is to correct sticking-out ears in new-born babies. There is also a reference to research on so-called "cot deaths", to add to my original advice not to put babies on their stomachs.

Two new appendices have been added. The first distinguishes between smacking and abuse, and includes helpful guidelines for disciplinary smacking, published in America in *Family Policy* by the Family Research Council, Washington DC. The second appendix discusses some of the options open to women to make their home their principal place of work; including paid work. Modern domestic amenities, computers and other "tools" have made it much more practicable and enjoyable than ever it was in the past, and it is now much more widely accepted that women with young children need and want to spend more time with them.

My own dear children have all grown up without, thank God, falling into any of the ghastly traps provided by drugs and promiscuity that ensnare many youngsters today. Even their teenage years passed without the horrors described by some people as being typical of this period of life. Of course, they had ups and downs in their emotions and were sometimes, quite frankly, peculiar; but a sound training in manners, consideration and, above all, conscience helped us all to cope and help each other. Plus the time-honoured advice my mother always used to quote, "Never let the sun go down on your anger".

Most families *do* make a good job of raising their children, and are loved and respected in return. Culturally, some take a rather negative view of the traditional family at present and like to pretend that it is fading away. It isn't! It is still the norm and the overwhelming majority of people come from one.

When it was first published in 1985, a critic described *Good Children* as so old-fashioned that it was positively radical, because it was against the child-centred approach that was so much in favour then. It is much less unfashionable now to say that it is an insult to women to expect them to be handmaidens to selfish, uncooperative children. It is also much more obvious to most people that it is not a good idea to raise children to believe that they only have rights and no duties or responsibilities. In the end, we all want what is best for children; that is what parents have always wanted, and that is the reason I wrote this book.

---

[1] See *The Psychological Care of Infant & Child* (1928) by John Watson. This was a best-seller by the so-called "father of behaviourism".

A frugal meal! Lynette and husband Ken, plus:
(far side, left to right) Matthew, Riffen, Sophie; (front) Oliver, William, Emma.

Oliver's wedding to Patricia – with all the family.

Introduction

*The Domestic Art seems to me as special and
as valuable as all the ancient arts of our race.*

– G K Chesterton

"Happy families are all alike; every unhappy family is unhappy in its own way". So says Leo Tolstoy at the start of *Anna Karenina* and it is a strangely true observation. The reason for this must be that the family, like almost any other sort of enterprise, has an internal dynamic which, when it functions well, is found to run on similar lines to all the others. When it fails, it does so for a dozen different reasons.

The details of this dynamic vary from one family to another but the underlying principles that govern it usually do not. It is like a domestic eco-system where the delicate balance between the competing members may seem fragile but, in reality, if they have been constructed according to traditional methods (that is, tried and tested ones), they will prove sturdy, durable and happy. These basic principles are, broadly: love, mutual respect, tolerance, co-operation, discipline, some freedom of movement and enough space for everyone to feel they can develop.

What makes the family the great feast of an enterprise that it is, is that, alongside these purely organisational qualities, there goes a deep and natural love that is born into the family with every child, regardless of how the parents initially thought of themselves or of one another. Thus love, with its ability to create tension and excitement as well as to cause suffering, is central to everything that goes on in a family, infusing it with life.

It is often said that the family is a microcosm of society and, in many ways, this is true. Certainly the family has in common with the real world, the fact that we mostly cannot choose those with whom we associate. Even though the married couples choose one another, no one else in a family has any choice about their relations. We arrive in this world to meet a collection of brothers and sisters, aunts, uncles, cousins and grandparents, whom we haven't chosen to know, and who become the closest persons to us. A large part of our lives thereafter is filled with the fascinating business of getting to know them over the years, and learning to relate to people who are not at all what we might have chosen for ourselves had we had the chance. How much more do we learn, therefore, from these intimate strangers, than we ever learn from those we choose, because of their compatibility, as friends or colleagues.

Of course, some aspects of family life change as technology, events, or new ideas change the society around it, but the central relationships are still remarkably the same. Ironically, it was only really the feminists who thought that women had no power over the hearts and minds of men in the past. Most of us have always known where the power lies in the family, and that women set the standards in the home. Just as we have always known that for every woman considered a piece of property by her husband there was a man considered a doormat by his wife. Our common sense tells us that no man ever really thought of women as chattels unless he could first have regarded his mother as one – which he could not.

Nor has the relationship between parents and children altered very much despite immense changes in society. Apart from the basic requirement of love and protection, the need for the child to be soundly educated in moral and social values by its parents can be seen even more clearly today. It is also obvious that this parental duty cannot be easily fulfilled by any other agency.

Even those changes which have occurred in our domestic tradition due to external circumstances have seldom been really radical, in that we have never lost the pattern of married men working full-time, which gives their wives a chance to devote a large part of their time to their homes and children.[1]

Today, we seem to be moving away from the rather prim, essentially middle-class ethic of Victorian times, which saw women in the home as mothers and nothing else. Many women like to do other work at the same time as bringing up children *both* because they need the money *and* because it gives them the stimulus of other interests. Now, changes in our industrial and commercial scene, brought about by innovations like computers and fax machines, plus a high level of comfort and convenience in the home, have combined to make home-centred work a much more viable proposition than it was in the recent past. Not only women, but men too are discovering a time-honoured use for their houses as workshops and offices, as well as a home for the family.

Furthermore, changes in employment practices are beginning, at long last, to take account of the fact that married women have a commitment to their home and family that must be accommodated. Such things as job-sharing, relocation of work to the home and more flexible hours, mean that many women are in a better position to be the primary carers of their children – and still earn some money.

However, in order to have the freedom, the confidence and the sheer energy to organise a fulfilling home life whilst bringing up children, it may be necessary to discard a lot of the advice given over the years by professionals who have often done very little child rearing themselves. Particularly that part of it which is called "child-centred". It is one thing for professional men and women – from the safety of their studies and offices – to hand out advice on childcare which involves doing everything your child wants. It is quite another to try to enjoy life and motherhood when encumbered by the dead weight of a philosophy which turns the mother into a pathetic, exhausted handmaiden to a child's every whim and wish.

Things were never like that in the days when men and women worked together in the home before the industrial revolution, and the family house contained not only the family and the business, but apprentices, ancient relatives and servants too. Nobody then spoke about "toddler tantrums", aggressive seven-year olds, rebellious twelve-year olds and disaffected teenagers. These are the creations of a relatively leisured class that sees itself as being able to solve the problems it has helped to create.

I have not dwelt overmuch on the painful subject of what fools these experts think housewives are. However, you will get an impression from the examples cited in the book of the kind of ridiculous and outlandish advice on childcare sometimes given to women, which would be unthinkable, for instance, to any audience of similarly competent men. The same spirit of contempt for women's judgement and experience underlies attempts by some professionals to make smacking children illegal. The fact that an overwhelming majority of parents throughout the ages have thought moderate physical correction of children is necessary, is simply discounted by professionals who believe that they alone know better.

I do believe that children need their mothers very much in their early years and that this need for love and attention does not cease just because they have started school. However, it is perfectly possible to be involved in a number of other activities, including making some money, whilst bringing up your children as long as you have two things. One of these is children who are accommodating – which is what this book is all about, hence the "good children" of the title. The second is a more positive attitude towards a domestic environment which has, for too long, been portrayed as a dreary and limiting prison. In her home a woman has premises, opportunities and, above all, freedom to pursue more dreams and schemes than is ever possible in most jobs. It is true that she needs ideas and examples, but these are beginning to come thick and fast as more and more women are branching out into home-based work that enables them to remain at the centre of family and community life.

For anybody to develop and find fulfilment in any situation, it is necessary to have a congenial atmosphere. That is to say, other people have to be accommodating and co-operative. The commonplace but unfashionable idea I am putting forward in this book is that children, who share the home, can be taught the values and behaviour necessary to create this atmosphere from the earliest age.

There are a handful of key factors that contribute to a state of harmony and well-being within a family regardless of the financial and domestic difficulties which most families experience from time to time. You will find out more about these simple and basic principles in the following pages.

In view of the fact that there are many women today who, for a variety of reasons, are bringing up children single-handed, it is worth mentioning that this situation, though sad, is not new. Although single-parenthood in its present form is a relatively new phenomenon, widowhood and women who are on their own with their children because of wars or husbands working away from home, are not. The circumstances surrounding the family can vary but the central situation remains the same. Despite the fact that fathers are unquestionably important to their children and share with women the responsibility of being a parent, women *can* successfully rear their children on their own if they have to, and have always been able to.

Of course it is true that, in the absence of a man, most of the responsibility for loving, teaching and disciplining the child falls upon the woman. Not surprisingly, many feel daunted when faced with this task – I would suggest they have no need to. The authority and resourcefulness required for bringing up children is not a question of education, strength or even stamina. It is a question of confidence, and that confidence is a quality which women intrinsically possess. It can be seen in their stance, their clothing and their demeanour when they decide to express it.

One only has to look at the photographs of an earlier age to notice that women of all classes displayed a calm confidence that showed itself in their large hats, elaborate dresses and jewellery, and indicated that they were people who were not intimidated by, or apologetic about, their roles and responsibilities. It is impossible to imagine their being harassed, abused or disregarded by their children. They might have lacked status or political clout in the social hierarchy, but within the family they were recognised as the powerful figures they were.

It is not coincidental that alongside a loss of confidence that has been induced by the unremitting denigration of the job of housewife and the role of mother, there has arisen the cultural insult of women everywhere being portrayed, even in daily newspapers, as sexually provocative, naked and vacuous: possessing neither heart, nor head, nor dignity. Such an iconography contains nothing of the quality or values of real femininity and is a visual slander that undermines all the serious work that women do.

This book is an argument, not to return to old values, but to re-state eternal ones. It is an argument on behalf of the work that women have always done well and that children will always need. The family has lasted as an institution because it is adaptable. It travels or it stays put; it survives in war, famine, poverty or plenty; it changes little in the course of twenty generations or it alters completely in one. The heart and soul of this adaptability is co-operation. Learnt by children from parents, it makes the family resilient, flexible, ingenious and more than a match for any institution which might seek to destroy it.

So I would like you to forget for a moment all the medical, psychological and media advice given in the past and come with me into an ordinary home where a tradition of child rearing has been carried on that would be recognisably the same as that practised by other women at almost any time in our history. It is based upon skill, techniques and experiences that people must have shared with each other for many generations, and its aim is to maintain a balance between a child's need for love and attention and a mother's need for respect, consideration and some space to develop herself at the same time as bringing up her family. She also needs to be appreciated by society for the contribution she makes for the good of all.

The underlying philosophy of this book is principally that children are born into the adult world of their parents and fit naturally into it; not the other way round. This accommodation with their parents' world is, for children, a necessary prelude to fitting into the wider adult world.

The "Good Children" of the title indicates two aspects of the same quality. It means that they are good to be with because they are amiable and co-operative. They are also "good" in the sense that they function well as children. That is with all the enthusiasm, curiosity, helpfulness and good cheer that has always been associated with a childhood happily lived and with the optimism and promise of the future.

---

[1] Melanie Phillips states in *The Sex-Change Society* (1999) that, contrary to popular myth, men do about 60 to 65% of all paid work.

The first few days

In most things it makes sense to start at the beginning, so we are going to pick up the story of bringing up children at the moment when first the little damp creature that you have just produced is put into your arms.

To me, whether the birth has been in hospital or at home, the atmosphere is the same mixture of emotion, elation and relief; the same incredible climax when suddenly another person is in the room and the man and woman who were there before become a *family*.

It is an amazing experience and one which no amount of repetition ever dulls, although quite probably mothers vary in their feelings towards it. Certainly not everyone experiences a rush of "maternal" feeling or even a great sense of achievement, but no one can fail to feel the most enormous relief at the physical consummation of the job and wonderment at the result.

It probably takes rather more experience of babies than one normally has with a first child to realise that the experience of birth has been quite an ordeal for them too, and that they really need to be held by loving arms and hear the sounds of welcome and delight to reassure them that everything is all right.

It does not really matter if you do not feel the "right" emotions and you cannot, in any case, always turn them on to order. Just something positive will do and an atmosphere of congratulation and joy.

The encouraging cries of the midwife whilst you were giving birth – which always sound like someone cheering on a tug-o'-war team – will at last have given way to less urgent instructions, intermingled with requests for tea, expressions of pleasure and gratitude and the welter of emotions that almost everyone feels at such times. They are the baby's first experience of human emotion, and I am sure they register somewhere in that tiny computer of a brain, and that they're important for him too.

After a few hours, a feeling of anti-climax, which so often follows upon periods of intense excitement, may have temporarily dimmed the lustre of the first positive response to the new baby. But by that time he will probably be fast asleep anyway, so it does not matter. Make the most of those first few moments of pure pleasure and relief and pass them on while you can.

A baby is usually very tired after the experience of the birth and all the muscular activity he has been subjected to. The same will apply to the mother, particularly if she missed a night's sleep before it. So the period before the feeding really starts is a natural and welcome lull. There is little to do but doze and wake again to the sheer pleasure of realising that it is all over and you actually have the baby at last.

This feeling of euphoria can quite easily go to your head, and I still remember with a groan how, after my last baby was born, I was eventually wheeled from the delivery room and on to the ward, chirruping to all and sundry, "I've got a baby! I've got a lovely little baby!" The other women looked at me with amused derision and said, "Yes dear, you always feel like that after your first. You'll get over it"!

At visiting time, when all the others crept in and clambered on the bed, I disappeared under the bedclothes feeling absolutely pink with embarrassment.

One often does not realise until after the baby is born that your milk does not "come in" until the third day; which means that if the birth is on Monday, it will be Wednesday at least before you can feed the baby properly. In the meantime you will suckle him just the same every four hours or so for a couple of minutes on each breast and the small amount of colostrum the baby obtains in this way is sufficient for what he needs.

Colostrum is a thickish, yellow substance that precedes the proper milk in your breast. It is a rich food for the baby and helps to evacuate the black "goo" that the baby has in his system as a result of his time in the womb.

There are some babies who just do not seem to realise that, according to the baby books, they are not supposed to be ravenously hungry from the word "go"; and they can be something of a problem to a new mother in the first few days.

They will go on screaming after you have given them what little you have to give, apparently unaware that some people are trying to get some sleep – like their mothers, for instance. In the end you may be weeping yourself, convinced that there is something wrong with you because, even at this early stage, you cannot do what is necessary for your child.

If the child is born at home, this is less of a problem, because midwives are less hide-bound by rules than are hospital nurses. They are, after all, in your environment rather than an institutionalised one, and they will see the problem at close quarters and make up a bottle to satisfy the baby and allow everyone to get some sleep.

Whilst you are in hospital, however, it may be a little more difficult to do this since some nurses are opposed to using a bottle now for whatever reason. They think it will cause insurmountable problems involving the milk supply not developing as it should; not to mention the baby turning against the breast after experiencing the joys of a large and obvious teat.

Their positive championing of the breast may be welcome, but it can have the unfortunate side effect of making it seem that breast-feeding is a very tricky and fraught business which the slightest thing can upset, rather than the simple and natural process that it is.

My own experience has been that if your baby is obviously hungry in the first few days before your milk supply is properly established, or even if he seems hungry and unsatisfied after a feed that has thoroughly emptied you, giving him a bottle *after* you have given him all you have does nothing to impair your milk supply. Nor does it mean that he will then reject the breast in favour of the bottle because he will always go for what is offered first when he is really hungry.

In the first few days after a baby is born, the most difficult thing to cope with may often be the unaccustomed lack of sleep. One can easily come to feel quite desperate at the seeming impossibility of ever getting a chance to sleep; and the more tired one gets, the greater the problem looms.

Once you have got the baby to go to sleep after his food, even if it is only for two or three hours, you feel so much better that everything else improves. Your confidence and optimism return and you can sit down and relax, which will do a great deal to encourage your milk to build up.

It is rest, routine and plenty of fluids which help your milk supply, plus the level of demand from the infant. But if, for some reason, it does not, it will not help to sit around staring in anguish at your screaming infant and wondering why it is that he does not seem to like you. Just top him up with whatever it takes to make him sleep for a good three hours.

Breast-Feeding

Perhaps the biggest practical change in baby care that has occurred has been the switch back from bottle-feeding to the breast, which I am concentrating on in this chapter simply because full and clear instructions are issued with every box of dried milk if you are going to bottle feed.

In the hospital in London where I had my first baby, it was assumed that everyone would bottle feed. When I told the nurse who automatically brought me a bottle that I intended to breast feed, she was astonished and, whilst congratulating me as if I was the first lucky woman for a generation to have discovered a use for the funny lumps we women all seem to have on our chests, told me that so many women *could not* breast feed that they scarcely took it into account.

And yet, looking around the ward at the other eleven women, they did not look to me like people who *could not* feed. On the contrary, they were all taking pills the size of horse tablets to dry up their milk, and some of them had their chests tightly bandaged to keep the dreaded milk away. They suffered agonies of discomfort for which they took more pills – and moaned and groaned all day.

It may be unfair to blame the medical profession entirely for the demise of breast-feeding that occurred at this time, but doctors certainly facilitated it by handing out suppressive pills. Neither did they seem to want to try and discuss with women their often irrational and unfounded reasons for not doing the obvious and natural thing.

Indeed, during the height of the fashion, some doctors and nurses seem to have had rather strange ideas on the subject themselves. I remember listening in a ward to a young doctor solemnly explaining to a woman that the reason so many of her sex could not breast feed was because their situation was similar to that of the domestic cow. This simple creature once had the power to be both fast and ferocious in order to protect her young, but domestication had robbed her of this ability. Similarly, because modern women wore brassières, sat at desks and occasionally used their brains, they had lost all ability to feed their young. It was lucky, he added as a profound afterthought. that science had filled the breach with such timely innovations as powdered milk and sterilisers. . .

Fearing that I would be unable to prevent myself from stuffing his stethoscope down his jumper if I did not say something, I asked him if that meant he could foresee a time when women's bosoms would wither and drop off!

But no, he did not foresee that, although he was prepared to predict that they would get smaller over the years to come. Not in his ward though. In his ward, as he spoke, there were eleven women whose sculptured chests would have done justice to the Venus de Milo, but none of them was breast feeding her baby – partly, at least, because he said that they *could not* do it.

Now that the fashion has passed in this respect, one can put the case for and against breast-feeding quite simply. If you are unable to or cannot bear the idea then don't. In every other case, do.

In the first place, it is very much easier since you do not have the bother of preparing and heating up the bottle, particularly at night, and the even greater bother of cooling it down to just the right temperature. Neither do you have all the trouble associated with the important business of sterilising everything, not to mention the considerable expense this involves.

Furthermore, you know that your milk has everything in it that the baby needs, as the human body has evolved this food for its young over millions of years. It is *human* milk and not milk that was designed to satisfy the needs of a four-footed animal that lives out its days in a field.

It is unlikely to make the baby either windy or constipated and, except in a very few exceptional cases, it will not disagree with him. Thin and watery as the milk appears, it is the very stuff of life to a baby and contains minute quantities of irreplaceable minerals, the importance of which are still not fully understood. Lastly, it helps to immunise the baby from a whole range of illnesses.

On the less practical side, the very position in which you hold a baby to feed is linked to an instinctive need for both of you. A midwife told me once that she had never seen a woman, whether left-handed or right-handed, who did not hold a baby with its head on her left side and over her heart. She thought it must be an instinct to place the baby where it can hear and be comforted by the heartbeat that it knows so well from its time in the womb.

Demand Feeding

Generally speaking, three hours is a useful minimum period to aim for between feeds because it is really the amount of free time that one needs to continue living a more or less normal and tolerable life. One needs to have time for a good chat, a good sleep, to take a bath or put the washing on.

For this reason, it is my personal feeling that "demand feeding" is a non-starter. This method goes in and out of fashion over the years and entails feeding the baby whenever he wants and without any overall pattern or routine. It always appears to me that for some reason, women who go in for it seem to have their babies *permanently* clamped to their chests like oversized limpets.

Whilst this is no doubt an exaggeration, one certainly does end up feeding more frequently, the reason for which can be seen if you transfer the demand-feeding principle to a later age. Imagine that you have a five-year old who is given a piece of toast upon waking in the morning and, thereafter, tasty snacks whenever he feels like it throughout the day. For a start it would be likely to create a habit of wanting to peck at food all the time which could be difficult to break. Secondly, he would never be hungry enough to eat a meal of a sufficient size to last him for a few hours. This is roughly the position with demand-fed babies. They are always nibbling and you are never free. Some women like this, of course, and would not want it any other way, but others find it a strain and would really prefer to have a more regular arrangement.

The only exception I would make to the assertion that demand feeding is a mistake is in the case of small or frail babies. Their little stomachs may be quite unable to hold enough to last long between feeds, and they may not be strong enough to feed for very long without getting tired and going back to sleep. It may well be a case of what the old wives used to call "nature's way": you worry so much over a small baby that you do not mind making terrific efforts, particularly at feeding him. You feel that if only he can put on some weight he will not look in such danger of fading away. Feeding helps to calm these often irrational fears and, indeed, small babies often do put on weight at an amazing rate which makes it all worthwhile.

On the other hand, with a solid, obviously well-fed infant, his very greediness can make you resentful of the demands made on you when you are feeling tired. A choice can develop between his love of food and your sanity, with you becoming very irritated as a result.

Feeding Routine

It is not too difficult to establish a mutually satisfactory feeding routine if you are like me and need some space between feeds. What happens, for instance, if once you are back home the baby starts crying half an hour, or even an hour, before you want him to? Well, for a start, you do not want to appear the moment he makes a noise because you do not want to teach him that crying immediately produces your anxious face over the side of the cradle. That would give him, in a surprisingly short time, an inflated sense of the importance of his crying which will ensure that, as a technique to get what he wants, he will use it frequently.

A few minutes after his starting to cry, you will approach cheerfully and full of encouraging noises, and you can distract him from his hunger for quite a long time by cuddling, rocking, walking around the garden or singing and making faces. Even tiny babies seem to appreciate being entertained or at least, they will lie in your arms peering dimly at you in a sort of stupefied silence for a proportion of the time you are trying to take up.

By this means you can bring them a little nearer to the time you are aiming for; this will serve to make them that bit more hungry which, in turn, will make them take enough to last longer before the next feed. Thus you gradually build up the baby's intake, a predictable routine and the calm and tidiness that good order brings.

Of course, if the baby cries with really anguished hunger before time, that is, with a harsh all-consuming cry, then there is nothing to do but feed him. It often happens that, in response to that cry, your own milk will come rushing in, so that you too have no choice but to go galloping over to him with a need comparable to his own. In any case, as long as you have an overall routine to guide you, which makes you feel roughly organised, it does not really matter how often you break your rules.

There is no need to feel that because you are breast-feeding you can never go out. All you need is a little manual breast pump from the chemist with which you can express your milk, and this can then be left in a sterilised bottle. The teat goes into the sterilising solution and you tell whoever is going to feed the infant to drop the teat into the boiling water with which they will heat up the bottle. This is both to remove the taste of the sterilising solution and to warm up the teat. As an alternative method, my daughters tell me that steam sterilisers are easier to use. A breast-fed baby may not accept very readily a cold, suspiciously smelly teat when he is used to a beautifully warm breast.

Speaking of which, it may be as well to remember that, since bosoms are a vital part of this arrangement, it is important to know how to look after them sensibly. Apart from the fact that a hefty infant suckling can make them very sore, there are some women who find the first few minutes of every feed uncomfortable. For them the delicate tissue of the nipple is very tender before a feed and when the baby first snaps on the breast in the rumbustious way that some of them have, there may be a burning sensation that only lasts a minute or so, but it can he enough to make you dread it.

This problem can be very simply overcome with the use of a nipple-shield. This invaluable piece of equipment is inexpensive and can be obtained from the chemist – it is simply a teat attached to a saucer-shaped disc. You put the disc over the nipple whence the teat sticks out like a bottle. It looks a bit outlandish, but the baby does not mind and will suck the teat and draw your milk through it. It is a slower way of feeding but you could, if you wanted, do a whole feed like that. Normally, after three or four minutes, the pressure on the breast is relieved and you can put aside the shield and feed properly without any discomfort.

The shield is also very useful at the first sign of any cracking or soreness of the nipple. If this happens one will often be told to lay off the breast for a couple of feeds to give it time to heal but this leaves you feeling so congested and lopsided that you want to walk with a limp! The use of the humble nipple-shield is a practical solution although it is not one that seems to be very much recommended at present. Most probably you will have to ask for it yourself rather than wait for a doctor or a nurse to suggest it.

Night Feeding

A tiny baby has no idea of night and day or of the passing of time. All he knows is that every three or four hours the pangs of hunger disturb him and he cries for food, regardless of the fact that everyone else is trying to sleep.

As a matter of fact, it is not nearly such a problem in reality as it would seem to be in contemplation, because a mother's sleep pattern changes considerably after she has had a baby. Even people like me, who tend normally to go to bed and faint every night and who never find getting up easy – even after seventeen hours' sleep – will find that a combination of heightened instincts, hormonal changes and the restlessness induced by being pregnant mean that getting up for the night feeds is not as much of a problem as they thought it would be.

When the familiar wail reaches your ears like a distant alarm, you hop quickly out of bed and collect the baby without pausing to change the nappy or the whole house will be awake. Keep a small piece of plastic handy to put under him if he is wet, and so back to bed.

Here is a little fashion that seems to have changed for the better recently. Not so long ago, it was considered reprehensible to feed a baby in bed and you were always advised to sit on a low, straight-backed chair to do the night feeds. The thinking behind this was, presumably, that you might suffocate the baby if you fell asleep and rolled over on to it. Actually, you will find that it is impossible to roll onto something like a baby held in the crook of your arm when you are lying down. Try it and see!

Some people have even become so far enthused with the idea of having the baby in bed that they advocate keeping him there all night. This is an idea which would seem easier to talk or write about than to put into practice. Two people trying to share a roomy bed with a small and elusive infant means that the mother, as usual, will have the devil of a time trying to keep track of him *and* get some sleep.

Practical experience will, I think, demonstrate that while you doze when feeding the baby, you do not sleep deeply because the responsibility of the child is always on your mind. Should you go to sleep like that you will awake later feeling very unrefreshed because of this underlying worry.

It is probably much better to feed the baby and doze, letting him take as long as he likes so that he will be well filled, before heaving yourself out to put him back, with a quick nappy change, into his cradle. Then you and your husband, who also has to be considered if he is in the bed too, can really relax and abandon yourselves to sleep.

Really the last thing to be said on the subject of breast-feeding is not practical but purely aesthetic. Anyone who has the chance to enjoy a baby at the breast with his eyes closed and every curve of his body expressing bliss – one tiny hand stroking your breast, the other tucked under your arm – will see human contentment at its most fulfilled. It is an image, I am sure, that even when you are old and grey and long past other loves, will cause you to curl your toes at the beauty of the remembrance.

Weaning and dining

The first stage of feeding a baby is establishing a mutually satisfactory routine for the early months when he will be having only milk, preferably his mother's. Once this has been established, feeding the baby becomes such an easy and pleasurable activity that there is no need at all to disturb him until you feel it is time to start weaning (at somewhere between three and six months, or even later).

Weaning is the process of varying the baby's diet to include solid food, which will be introduced gradually until such time as his four-hourly milk feeds have given way to the more or less adult pattern of three meals a day – still, of course, including a good deal of milk.

Exactly when to start weaning will probably be suggested to you by the baby's attitude towards his food. He may be a big baby and be obviously interested in food. He may take a great liking to rusks and anything else he can chew or suck: or he may be rather bored with feeding at the breast and fool around instead of applying himself with the single-minded devotion he once showed. You may even find that he tries to take the food out of your mouth when you are having a mid-morning snack because he has worked out for himself that eating can be fun.

It is probably a good idea to wait until the peak of a hot summer is past before starting to wean, so that there is no risk of contamination to what he eats. It is also not a good idea to start weaning if the baby is at all unwell, for the obvious reason that you do not expect anyone to embark on a new adventure when they are not feeling at their best.

If the baby is under three months old and quite happy with breast-feeding, there seems little reason to consider weaning at all. It is good for them to build up their security and therefore their confidence, with an effortless way of doing things that continues unchanged for at least that time.

One usually starts weaning with one of the many proprietary baby-cereals since they are sufficiently bland and milky to be acceptable to him. At which feed you choose to make the introduction will depend upon your own observation of the child.

As a rule, most babies will be too hungry at the morning feed to have much patience with any attempt to slow them down with a silly old spoon. On the other hand, if you give it at lunch-time when he is more relaxed, you may find that it makes him sleep like a log for hours on end and messes up the evening schedule. The evening, if you are not too busy with the rest of the family, can be a good time to start since the extra "weight" of the solid food certainly does help to make some babies sleep very soundly for a long time.

Whether you offer your little teaspoonful of cereal at the start of a meal or at the end will have to depend upon the circumstances, but you should not be surprised if he does not think much of it anyhow. Some babies make no problems; they just open their mouths and in it goes. Others are suspicious, resentful even, as if they suspect you of trying to poison them and they can set their little jaws fast against the intrusion of the spoon.

In circumstances like these it is a good idea to transfer the baby's attention from the spoon as a means of feeding him to the spoon as a super-powered aircraft! "Zoom, zoom", you will go, hopping the spoon-plus-cereal out of the cup and making it scream across the sky *à la* Biggles. As it goes past his mouth it will tip out its contents via his slack lower lip in an almost non-committal way and he will hastily gulp it down before fixing his eyes back on the cup to watch you conjure up another plane.

You may have to do this, with variations, for several meals until you have given him a taste for the food. When that happens he will not need further inducements to make him eat, although it is a useful game to fall back on if ever his appetite is lost through being out of sorts.

The usual way to start introducing solids to a baby is by giving them at only one meal a day to start with; gradually increasing to two and three meals depending on how quickly he takes to it. If you just bear in mind that you are changing his diet fairly radically, you will make the change as gradually as he can accommodate. It may be a good idea to keep to the same, or at least similar, foods at first because there may be some flavours he just will not like, and you do not want to risk hitting on one of these too early.

Texture is another matter altogether, and many babies hate anything crumbly or lumpy even when they are tolerant of quite strong flavours. So you may have to blend, mash or sieve everything for some time after he has accepted the idea of solids.

On the subject of strong flavours, it is worth making a passing mention of fads like giving unsweetened yoghurt as the only food for a newly weaned infant. It may be good for them, although I must confess that it surprises me any infant can be induced to accept anything so sour and unlike his mother's milk. It probably goes to show that you could get a baby to eat frogspawn off a spoon if you persisted for long enough!

However, there is one disadvantage to unrelieved yoghurt and this is that when you come to try natural food, like fruit for instance, the baby reacts in disgust and spits it out. You then have to undertake a sort of secondary weaning to get him off the taste for the very sour and on to less strong flavours.

When you have got your child well used to solid food and a spoon, which may take two or three months to achieve, you can begin, again very slowly, to give him portions of the family's meals, well-mashed or blended in a liquidiser and with the seasoning left out (you must not use any salt when cooking for infants as it can poison them). There are some meals which are suitable for babies without any modifying, such as cauliflower cheese, shepherd's pie, macaroni cheese, soups and stews. Even if you are having something that a baby cannot easily eat, such as a roast, you can mash a little of the vegetable with the gravy to make a portion for him.

There are literally dozens of different varieties of tinned meals for babies and they make a pleasant change for mother and baby from time to time. However, they are an expensive way of feeding a child and, in nutritional terms, they are not necessary.

Eating Together

Eating the same food as the rest of the family has the advantage of making the child less likely to be choosy or awkward about his food. Babies, like older children, have a great desire to do what the big people around them are doing so it is a good idea, as soon as they are big enough, to let them eat with the rest of the family.

When they are happily seated in their baby-chair as part of a group at the table, they are not the centre of your attention and so can get on with the eating without thinking about putting on displays of temperament for your benefit. It becomes an interesting and unselfconscious occasion for them and consequently is more likely to be free from that element of struggle which sometimes develops when they are fed on their own.

There are always one or two things that even a baby does not like and it is better not to hassle over whatever they are, but to drop them for the time being. There is no single food that is so important that a substitute cannot be found quite easily so that, although it is an inconvenience if a baby does not like egg, cheese or banana since they are easy foods to prepare, it does not matter and will probably pass away in time if you do not make too much fuss about it.

When the baby is eating solid food regularly, his diet will still need to include plenty of milk and, indeed, you may well have continued to feed him yourself. However, if you have given up breast-feeding you should use your own judgement of the child to decide how best to give him his milk. Certainly a cup is a quick and easy way, particularly if he is now eating his meals in a chair, but a good many babies love sucking and, what is more, they have a very strong inclination towards it. So, if you put them entirely onto a cup because they are now on solid food, this unsatisfied sucking instinct will take the form of voraciously sucking their fists, even between mouthfuls at mealtimes and sucking their thumbs, fingers, bits of cloth and anything else that comes their way.

If you have a baby like this, who obviously gets lot of satisfaction from sucking, then let him have a bottle at least in the mornings and evenings or with his fruit-juice during the day. Cups are a very efficient way of getting drink down him but there are times when he wants a drink to last longer than half a minute. There is no way that you can stretch the emotional satisfaction of a cup so that it lasts for ten minutes – which may be what you need to satisfy a baby in whom old habits die hard.

Throughout childhood, and indeed throughout life, the basic ingredients of good eating habits are regularity and conviviality. Eating between meals only blunts the appetite and can make a child more choosy when it comes to mealtimes. It also encourages him to put on more weight than he needs. If you have a child who gets peckish between meals, keep a store of fresh or dried fruit handy, or vegetables like carrots and celery, to help him last the distance.

Children are by nature company seekers. They have to be so from the very beginning when they look blindly for their mothers as a source of food. This need for others is widened by inclusion in a family circle which is, in itself, a microcosm of the wider world but on their scale. Mealtimes are important occasions for children since they are built round one of their principal interests and are a natural, unselfconscious setting in which to learn how to listen to others and to talk.

Of course bad habits can creep into mealtimes like bickering, for instance, and trying to settle disputes just because you are all present for a change. For my own peace of mind and enjoyment, I always absolutely forbid any quarrelling at table on the completely arbitrary grounds that it is an insult to the cook!

So is complaining about the food of course, instead of just being grateful for it. I often had occasion to remind my children – and husband – of Samuel

Johnson's wife turning on him one evening when he was saying grace: "Nay,
Sir, hold! – Do not make a farce of thanking God for a dinner which you will
presently protest not eatable."

A fine woman, Mrs Johnson, and a lady who knew the respect due to her
for the job!

Sleeping

Eating and sleeping are the two predominant features of a new-born baby's life and between them they occupy almost all his time. If his eating habits are of primary interest to the baby, his sleeping habits might well be said to be of equal interest to the mother since, when the child sleeps, she too can rest.

Both these activities are instinctive to a baby and are therefore perfectly natural. However, the setting we bring them into may not be natural and this in itself can cause certain familiar problems.

Most people will have been into homes where the presence of a new baby is indicated by certain unnatural restrictions.

"Can you use the downstairs loo – the baby is asleep upstairs."

"Keep the telly down – you'll wake the baby."

"You can't play in the house – you know how easily the baby wakes up." How does this unnatural state of affairs come about when it is plain, from his recent history, that sleeping is something a baby can do anywhere, anytime and anyplace? How else would he have managed to sleep in the womb?

Tolerance of Noise

It is known from the many studies of the life of a child in the womb that cramped living quarters are only one of the inconveniences he has to live with; he has also endured a high level of noise since conception.

There are the rumblings and gurgles of his mother's stomach; the rushing and pumping of the bloodstream, faint noises from the world outside and the steady, pervasive drub-drub of the heartbeat. All these noises are close to him too, not a room or a street away but in his ears for every minute of the day and night. How quiet the world must seem when he is born into it; how deathly still and quiet compared to what he has been used to.

Seen against this background, it is not at all surprising that when he is in a room, noisy with adults and other siblings, he does not bat an eyelid. Noise is the context in which he has developed so far and it does not disturb him.

Imperviousness to it, therefore, is his natural state at this time and if you build upon this fact purposefully, you will ensure that it stays that way. This is not a difficult thing to achieve except that, in the superior living conditions that many people enjoy today, it may not happen without some planning.

Let me give an example of what I mean. When we had our first baby, we lived in a two-roomed flat in London, just off Oxford Street, in the parish of Soho. We had a kitchen-cum-workroom for my husband and a bed-sitting room for everything else.

So when I brought Emma home from the hospital there was nowhere else to put her except in her wicker cradle, on a small table at the foot of the bookcase. Had you asked us at the time, no doubt we would have said that it was a great shame she did not have a room of her own and, had I been offered the choice, I would certainly have said that I would have preferred a properly equipped nursery, complete with gingham curtains, polished wood floor and clean, tasteful toys.

In fact, like countless families before us, we were too poor at this stage of our married life to have such a room and so the baby came into what we had. Friends and relations came to see us at all times of day and evening, my husband sang loudly as usual at his drawing board, I practised my banjo. Life had to go on.

One night we had a party and a friend of a friend, who was looking for something in the bookcase, suddenly jumped a foot in the air and, pointing a quivering finger at the basket said, "My God! You've got something alive in there!"

"Yes, you nut, it's a baby! Just watch where you put your drink."

"But it's asleep – in all this noise! Is it deaf?"

"No, just used to it, I suppose.

"It's incredible, it really is. What a *good* baby!"

But it was not really incredible, just extremely old-fashioned. In the old days, as one can see from innumerable old prints of cottage interiors, the baby was always kept in the warmest room. The one with the fire in it, the living room where everything happened and all the company came.

Our material circumstances improved somewhat and by the time numbers five and six were born, we actually had a room into which the baby could have gone. By then, however, we knew that the baby's place was right where it was all happening and I always had a cradle in whichever room was most used, as well as a night-time one in our bedroom.

Keeping up the Tolerance

Babies like noise around them and – apart from sudden, loud noise – they are both comforted and entertained by it. When you first come home from hospital, the problem is seldom that there is too much noise; it is far more likely to be that there is too little to keep up their tolerance.

So, when you first come home from hospital, if the house is too quiet, put the baby in a cradle in the living room and turn on some music or the radio. You want him to get used to a certain kind of domestic noise and to a certain level of it so that he will not expect absolute quiet in order to sleep.

It is nice to simply stand and admire this new person and to show him off to callers without having to wake him up. You can talk, play records and even vacuum the floor without disturbing him – though you may need to start it up on the other side of the room. Nothing will bother or disturb him if that is what you have done from the start.

Babies are such creatures of habit that if you bring them into a quiet environment, you will find yourself creeping about the place and, within a couple of weeks, they too will have lost their imperviousness to noise and will be disturbed by every sound.

Comfort

There is not only something very natural and comforting for the baby in being within your sight and sound but for the mother also there is a benefit. It is, after all, something rather phenomenal that has happened to her. Without having had to acquire special skills, diplomas or qualifications, she has been able to produce this little human being. She has created a miracle of sophisticated engineering that is her responsibility and yet it is quite beyond her scope in any rational sense.

This sense of wonderment and achievement, deep and unexpressed as it often is, has as its other side a negative feeling of inadequacy – of doubt at ever being able to handle this superb creation properly.

It took me a long time to get used to the fact that my babies were strong enough to survive by themselves. There had been innumerable occasions in my childhood when we had rescued birds from our various cats and had fed them all evening, only to find them the next morning, dead in the nest we had made for them in a box.

Perhaps, because of these youthful experiences, I retained a fear that anything small and defenceless was also very fragile. When the new baby had been asleep for some time, particularly overnight, I would be seized by a mortal fear that she had died and would go rushing to her in a sudden agony of anxiety, to listen to the sound of gentle breathing. It is at times like this that the advantages of always having your baby near you become apparent and it certainly does help when the mean old clouds of doubt cross your still volatile spirits.

Company

After the first few weeks of almost constant sleep between feeds, the baby will be awake for longer periods and he will be content to lie and gaze around, listening to all the sounds and moving his hands. Later on he will watch you moving around the room, the shadows on the wall, the sunlight and the many quiet incidents of domestic life.

Often small babies cry, not for food or because of discomfort, but for company. They love to be part of a scene where people talk to them as they go about their business and give them things to look at and play with.

They only expect to be picked up all the time if you have got them into the habit by responding too readily to any crying. This often comes about because they are kept upstairs in their own room all the time. Neither they, nor their mothers, fathers or siblings, see enough of each other and this unsatisfied yearning takes the form of rushing to pick them up the moment they open their eyes and cry. This they will then do with increasing regularity.

By having the baby as part of the living-room furniture, so to speak, you keep him closely associated with your own routine and this is an easy and painless way of getting him into the 24-hour routine that you want. Somewhere between his fourth and his eighth week, he will, with luck, start to drop one or both of his night-time feeds – you want them to be the ones after midnight and not before.

This is encouraged by having evenings which are sociable and relaxed affairs with the baby in your company; perhaps lying on the sofa while you are watching television or entertaining friends. He will watch and listen and tire himself out quite nicely so that by the time you are ready for bed, he will be too, and a good feed should send him off for hours. With any luck it will not be long before he is letting you sleep at least until six in the morning.

As to the question of how long you can continue to have a baby constantly "about your person" as you might say, the answer is probably for as long as he will fit into a cradle.

Emma was quite a small baby and continued in her cradle until almost a year old, when we moved to a cottage in the country and she went straight into a cot at night. If we had had the room, she probably would have started to go upstairs to her cot once she was sleeping less and had settled into a three-meals-a-day routine at about eight months old. But it did not seem to matter much to her anyway and after tea at six-thirty, she would remain happily asleep throughout the evening and night regardless of what was happening in the room around her.

There was a brief period at about seven months old when teething problems caused her to be restless in the evenings. I retain fond memories of her at this time, sitting with a bottle of juice in her hands among all the long legs stretched out by the table. People shouting and laughing and she serenely playing with their shoelaces: so much a part of the scene and yet in her own little world.

Travel

Babies who sleep well regardless of what is going on around them are also a great asset when you want to travel or go visiting. As I keep mentioning, babies form habits very quickly and easily and a quiet room in a silent house becomes a necessity to a child that has experience of only that. Therefore, they will not be able to sleep on trains or in strange places where the noise levels are different from what they are used to. So they will cry and fret even though they are very tired.

Day and Night Routine

Once they are in the routine of three meals a day and are into a cot, they will still very likely need to sleep a good deal. Babies vary considerably in this respect, and some will want a mid-morning nap as well as a longer sleep after lunch. Most of them will be quite happy going to bed at about six-thirty or seven o'clock, but if you find they are not tired then, you will probably need to stop one or both of their day-time rests.

A problem that sometimes arises over the night-time sleep is connected with the fact that, when you first put the baby down to sleep, he may cry. This is just a way of "unwinding" for the baby and is a kind of release from the tension of being awake. He cries, sometimes loudly, for a few minutes and then drops off. He does not really want you to pick him up again which only confuses and irritates more. Just leave with some soft, comforting but final words and a few strokes of the head and, in a few minutes, he should be fast asleep.

The long hassle with bedtime that some parents experience often starts with their not recognising this tired crying for what it is and trying to coax the child to sleep without it. They end up pacing the floor with the child for hour after hour, or bringing him downstairs again in the hope that he will eventually be tired out sufficiently to be slid into bed without his noticing.

Of course this means that the child comes to know that all he has to do in order to be picked up is to cry, and so he will do that whether or not he is tired and the family's evening peace is disturbed by a bad-tempered child who just does not know what to do with himself.

It is better not to get involved with anything so fraught as this but to regard bedtime as the end of the day and that is that! As long as you know that the baby is not ill or in pain, you know that he is ready for bed in the evening and will go quite happily if there is no choice.

If a baby has got into bad habits whereby he cries every time you put him to bed and you have to keep popping in to quieten him, you can put an end to it quite simply by ignoring his crying for a few nights, after which time the message will get across that you mean business and are *not* going to come in. Hope is the fuel on which the crying runs, and when that is removed the crying will stop.

Actually, there are always odd days when a child really does want to be comforted at night because he is uncomfortable, cold or sickening for something, but it is only possible to identify these cases of genuine need if the child does not make a fuss every evening.

Babies who sleep well wherever they are become children who do the same. They become robust sleepers who do not require an unbroken chain of sleep in order to achieve a good night's rest, but can easily accommodate being woken up and will then sleep again without difficulty.

This can be very useful when you are beginning to leave off nappies and want to "pot" them last thing at night. In fact, it is always useful since there are so many things which disturb children's nights from tummy aches and coughs to nightmares – and, later on, someone having to wake them up to ask where they left your bicycle keys!

The hope is, of course, that they will become adults who sleep just as soundly and easily. I do not see why not since many childish habits have a way of lasting a lifetime, so it is just as well if they are good ones.

Training

I am going to use the word "training" for the subject of this chapter, despite the connotations it has for some people of dogs going through hoops, because I cannot think of another word that will do. The word "education" is used in this book to mean formal learning such as that acquired through literature, religion, art and school which leaves me free to use "training" for all the other things a child is systematically taught by his parents about the world and how to behave in it. It has been out of fashion for so long now that many people will think this chapter is all about potties; so let me reassure them that only the last part is!

The very last thing I want to do is give the impression that there is only one sort of pleasant family life, and that one ought to "train" one's children to fit it. "One man's meat is another man's poison" in this as in many other things, and all families are as different as the individuals who comprise them.

We all recognise when people are happy and fulfilled together, with no one excluded from the feeling of well-being. Such shared happiness does not depend upon having any particular style or standard of living but rather on a quality which underlies all good living of whatever fashion; and that is *consideration*. It may seem a small thing but it is, in fact, an active form of imaginative kindness which affects profoundly both the way a child thinks and how he behaves.

People do tend to become more considerate as they grow older and as social life imposes its laws upon them. However, it is when children are young that mothers need all the kindness and consideration they can get from their families if they are to avoid feeling undervalued and overworked when they are tired and when the endless routine seems just too much.

It is then that the comparatively small things a child does to help or please really make a difference in practical or emotional terms. A special effort to clean and tidy a room not only means one less job for mother, but it produces a feeling of being helped and appreciated – because you have been thought about – out of all proportion to the size of the job.

It is therefore important to teach children how to do jobs and relate them to what *needs* to be done rather than what *they* want to do. It is equally important to teach them a personal standard of behaviour that is not varied according to their assessment of what they can get away with. There can be few things more horrible than the person who has a sliding scale of manners depending on one's relative importance in his eyes, but such a habit starts very young and, indeed, is already being perfected by the child who treats his mother worse than he treats anyone else.

It is because children are so easy to train that it is important to undertake this task consciously and with some purpose, otherwise your very lack of conviction will unwittingly train them in another way. Thus, most children will become thoughtless and selfish if they are allowed to do what they want all the time and, although you may not intend it, that is what lack of training will produce.

Take the case of children helping in the house, for example. Most people would probably like to have children who see themselves as members of a family group and not as honoured guests to be waited on and served by the adults. Apart from the fact that "many hands make light work", the unselfish attitude of a child who helps with the chores is infinitely preferable to the sort who thinks that only *they* have the right to be without dull jobs; but this does not come naturally, it has to be trained.

Such attitudes to helpfulness need to be consciously cultivated at a very young age, so that it becomes second nature to a child; for instance, to clear away the plates after a meal, instead of just walking away and leaving the work for someone else.

A child can start being helpful when very young by putting away his toys when he has finished with them at the end of the day and picking up clothes and books off the floor. It is a pleasant little game for a toddler to help around the house and, in time, he will come to appreciate that everything has to be done by someone, and that looking after a household is a shared thing.

Apart from anything else – and I think this is very important – such habits of activity help to create an energetic attitude to life. I have known several lazy and slovenly children who, when they were older, never seemed to be able to get things done without much pain and a feeling of effort, and yet they were not lacking in physical energy. They had just never been given enough to do, and their capacities for hard work were small. Moreover, a habit of inertia had developed which they would probably have to wrestle with all their lives.

For an example of negative training, albeit an unconscious one, just think of those adolescents who have never had to do anything useful in the house. You ask them to wash up for you, because everyone is involved in some enterprise or other, and they are not only slow and incompetent, they are embarrassed. They have been thoroughly trained to feel that such a useful and practical skill is no concern of theirs, even though they can never know when a time might come when they would need it.

Telling the Truth

For a more subtle example of simple training, consider the question of honesty and lying. All things being equal, children are very honest and will say exactly what they believe to be the truth. Sometimes this can he very awkward and all parents will be able to recall the "Why has Auntie Alice got such a red nose?" type of question which they ask at just the wrong moment. Or our friend's little boy who was hovering round a visitor when he was given a drink. When his dad asked him what he wanted he said, "Well, you said Tony drinks like a fish and I just wanted to see him do it".

One never wants to discourage honesty, although children have to learn tact and kindness as well, but in family life, there are occasions when being truthful for a child is not easy. For example, if something has been broken and you ask in a fury who did it, you cannot be surprised if, in the interests of survival, a child denies it. By any common-sense standard he would be foolish to bring down wrath at its hottest upon himself when a simple disclaimer could avert the danger.

What you have done, in such circumstances, is to put the price for telling the truth too high, and the child will probably lie in consequence. What you have to do is to wait until you have cooled down completely and then explain to the child that you *do* get annoyed sometimes when things are broken but that it is not really important. What *is* important is the truth, and that is why you want to know it and why you will not be cross with him.

You thus set up the truth between you as a standard to be loved and sought after and not something that is lost in a welter of angry words and tears. The child will understand why you got cross because he feels the same way about some things and he will know also that you understand why he lied at the time. Nothing need be hidden then, and speaking the truth becomes something to be desired, an aspect of reconciliation and not the signal for calamity.

It is salutary too for parents to look again at their own deficiencies of temper in the light of the effect they obviously have upon their children. It is often the first time that young parents realise that self-control is not only an abstract virtue but, when you have children, it is a real duty.

However, a good example from parents in the matter of self-control and manners, though helpful, is not in itself enough. One has only to consult one's experience to know that the last few years have produced many children of kindly and polite parents whose liberal good manners have yet produced children who are extremely rude to them.

It appears from this that it requires something more on the part of parents than simply being civilised themselves to prevent a child from developing a habit of being unpleasant when he does not get his own way, and abusive when he is angry. The child has to know that, at all times, you not only expect politeness but you positively *insist* upon getting it.

Politeness makes for civilised dealings with your children – which makes family life that much easier and more pleasant for everyone. It also helps children to absorb and understand that the way you treat all people, and how you talk to them, is very important.

You want your children to be polite, not just to strangers or to those in authority, but to friends and, most particularly, to members of their own family. You want, in other words, their good manners to be an integral part of their personalities and not just a superficial social veneer that is applied to impress only certain people.

A polite child does not have to be an insipid and revolting little "goody-goody" always trying to please adults with winning ways. Basically, he is one who is trying to show kindness to others and, though to start with it may only be a form of words, in time it will become a habit of expression that has a gentling effect on what he says and does.

It is not as difficult as it may sound to teach children good manners since most of the hard work will have been done when they were very young. Then, as they grow up, they will have acquired a habit of moderating their speech, even when they are angry, which is a solid basis for developing self-control.

A polite way of talking is so important within a family because of the number of individuals living in close proximity and the fact that there is more than one generation present in that mix. There are bound to be many occasions, quite apart from day-to-day irritations, when children will quite rightly challenge your way of doing things. Many old rules outlive their usefulness, and children are likely to notice these before you, since they are often the subject of them.

A child who comes to you with a coherent and affable statement of his point of view can be quite sufficient to make you accept it. It is just as important for parents to talk things over with their children in a civilised way since flexibility is not something which normally increases with age. Many parents need to be prised away from old and fondly-held habits and attitudes by their children, and it is one of the pleasures of a growing family that one does, indeed, hear new arguments about old problems from the children. Even if their experience only leaves the adults in a better position to argue the case, it is very stimulating to have to do so occasionally and it flatters and benefits the children to feel that they can discuss the rules and philosophy by which the household lives.

So when, you may ask, do you consciously start to train a child in anything? The answer is, as soon as he is old enough to communicate with you and so to learn – and that is very young indeed. There is a sense in which the very earliest feeding and sleeping habits are a matter of training also, but we will set these aside since they have been discussed earlier.

As a baby grows out of early infancy, so his observation and interest in the world around him develops. By the time he is several months old, he will be strong enough to sit up and reach for things around him and to test them with hands and mouth. This routine exploration goes on no matter what the child is doing, and everything is given the same treatment, whether an inanimate old shoe or a real live cat! So you have to be careful about what is left in their vicinity.

A baby sitting on his mother's knee will use the same learning technique with her, and will put his fingers in her mouth, fascinated by the warmth and the wall-to-wall teeth. He will pull her nose from side to side to see if it will come off and try to feel her eyes to see why they move. If the baby is the gentle and sympathetic sort, wrinkling your face and showing pain when he is rough will be sufficient to make him feel concern and so lead him to be more gentle.

However, a more aggressive infant might well enjoy the sense of power he gets from being able to produce such a result and he will do it more. It is, alas, not the case that all babies will be overcome with remorse seeing that their actions produce symptoms of distress. There are many children who are in no way abnormal or even particularly nasty, but who take a mischievous delight in producing such a reaction. They do not, after all, really know what they are doing, only that their actions produce a rather interesting facial expression and this will be enough to make them continue. With them you have to take a firm line and indicate, very positively, that they must not do it.

Whichever type of child you have, the result will be the same, and they will have learnt that certain kinds of roughness have to be avoided either because it can be seen to cause pain or because mother does not allow it! If you wanted to give a pretentious title to such a natural process, you would call it "training", and that is what we are talking about.

Most children aged between ten months and two-and-a-half years cannot speak properly in sentences and yet they understand very well most of what you say to them. They are mobile, quite strong and with powerful likes and dislikes. They are well aware that there are different ways of getting what they want. This is the time when any child with spirit and an interest in life will lay claim to everything he sees. He can open the fridge, reach the telephone, take down books and get into your handbag, fiddle with knobs and shake out the contents of jars and boxes.

It is up to you *then* to lay down your demarcation lines so that he understands them and, in consequence, knows where he stands in relation to what he can and cannot do.

In the first place it has got to be said that your child needs to be acquainted with the word "no" at least from the time when he first begins to crawl. There have been differing opinions expressed about the necessity of this short and useful word, and some people have thought that to use it gives children a negative attitude to life. Such logic is lost on me, I am afraid, since in practice one sees both the practical necessity for it and how positive and interesting it is to a child.

You will notice, for instance, that your child will often return to something that makes you utter the warning "no" because he finds it intriguing to test the repetition. It arouses positive emotions too, such as interest at why this object or situation is different from that one, annoyance as to why this one is not allowed and satisfaction at learning exactly what you mean by "no" and at the predictable communication between you.

A child has to learn that there are "no" areas in the world as well as "yes" ones. Indeed, for him to believe otherwise would be a real threat to safety and survival. A slightly more cautious approach to new and strange things is introduced into a child's mind which is infinitely preferable to a reckless confidence that leads a child to think he can do what he likes without any ill effect or danger.

When they are first mobile, children will spend many months testing out these "yes" and "no" areas with great enthusiasm and absorption. Scuffling up to something old or new and putting out an urgent hand for it before looking round to get your response. They learn for themselves surprisingly quickly what they can and cannot do and then they can use their own experience to evaluate a new situation. When, for example, they discover a pot or container which has something in it, they will not immediately empty the contents on the floor, but will thump down on their bottoms, clutching the article to their chest, and will then put it carefully on the ground, take off the lid and peer cautiously inside, knowing that, in general, you prefer contents to remain where they are.

It is not only a great satisfaction for them to know that they are learning about things, but giving them the means to censure their own actions enables them to be self-reliant, which is good for their self-confidence.

The alternative to this kind of strategy is to have everything that is valuable, breakable, decorative or expensive out of reach of the child, which means that no one can enjoy the beauty and interest of them. The place they live in thereby comes to look more like the guard-room of an army detention centre than a home, and everyone suffers.

There is certainly no doubt that once your child has learnt the "done thing" in your own home, both you and he are much more free. Instead of the exhausting business, which one too often sees, of a mother having to keep tabs on a child for every minute that he is in someone else's house or shop, you can be fairly certain that he will not attempt to do in unfamiliar surroundings what he is not allowed to do at home. And it does not worry or inhibit him in the least, you may be assured, because it is much nicer for him to be happily occupied with what he knows is allowed rather than to be blundering about from one disaster to another with mother following behind apologising distractedly whilst prising his hands off the china, and other people's food, and putting back books and CDs.

When a child does know, more or less, how to amuse himself at home and when he is visiting without causing undue trouble, the world is a very welcoming place. People appreciate an amiable and sensible little child so much that they go out of their way to be pleasant to him. They establish friendly communication with the child which causes him to see the world as benign and himself as an accepted part of it.

It is true that, when they are older, children have to learn that not all people are to be trusted, but warning is only appropriate when they are old enough to be out on their own. As the *Plowden Report* on education remarked back in the 1960s, "You have to teach faith before you cast doubts". That is the right order in which to lay down the basis for a happy and confident attitude towards the world.

When these friendly channels of communication are opened up between your children and others they become, in time, the means by which everything you teach them is tried out on other people and in another place. Indeed, it can be quite irritating to see the gusto with which they will help to weed someone else's garden or clean out cupboards when such home-taught chores are performed with somewhat less enthusiasm for you.

However, they are all skills which they can perform well or badly for others whilst experiencing an environment other than their own. When she was about seven, our second daughter, Sophie, used to go round to a neighbour's house and clean her shoes, since the old lady could not distinguish between the different colours of polish. In return for this chore she used to read to Sophie from *Punch* while she worked. It was a curious arrangement since Sophie probably did not do the shoes terribly well – but on the other hand, she could not have understood very much of what was read either. But it was an arrangement that suited them both and it developed into a more useful relationship later on.

Little Emma, as a teenager, visited a blind old lady of ninety-five whose memories of her life before the first World War were not only the only ones she had, but were as clearly recollected as if they happened yesterday. It was an education for Emma, more vivid than many hours in a history class, to talk about what it was like to live in those days – how hard they worked, how far they walked and how much fun they had with the simple pleasures and relative poverty of the times.

Even dear old Riffen, third son, and afflicted with a noise problem, found somewhere to go to be an independent man. When I say "a noise problem", I mean that he was the kind of boy who even *thought* noisily and who, as a little boy, had the distinction of being able to fall over from almost any position – even when he was standing still. My husband used to say that he was a natural barrow-boy, which may be just right. Certainly everything he did, though it be well-planned and carefully executed, was attended by a terrible commotion.

We got used to it, and to the phenomenon that if there was the most appalling crashing and banging going on upstairs, it was likely to be Riff making his bed or tidying his pencil-box. And so we all thought he would be at least 35 before anyone voluntarily invited him to visit them. Then one day he returned from the car-park behind our house to say that he had met a lady who wore her glasses upside-down and wanted him to come and brush her dog.

It all turned out to be true and the dear lady, who was almost a hermit living further down our terrace, wore her glasses upside-down because they were more comfortable that way and loved Riffen coming in to groom her dog. Bless her heart! She was almost totally deaf!

This widening of a child's social experience is valuable and enjoyable to them, not least because they are making their way by their own efforts and personalities. The fountainhead of all their resources at this time is the family and they will bring back to it all they see and learn elsewhere. It is a completely two-way process, since what they learn at home quickly becomes what they have to give outside of it and vice-versa.

Their early training so quickly becomes a part of a child's personality that you are no longer consciously aware of laying down any patterns of behaviour, or of training them in anything in particular. In fact, after about the age of six or seven, you are merely keeping in trim manners and sensitivities laid down earlier, with the added help of being able to talk about them and explain some of the reasons for doing things.

It is well worth the effort – if that is what you find it – of training your child in these simple, civilising ways, since small habits which are laid down early grow with the child until they become a very large part of his personality.

It is just one of the advantages of such a systematic approach that parents, as well as everybody else, come in the end to take pleasure from what most people mean by "a well brought-up child".

Potty Training

Having acknowledged in the first paragraph of this chapter that when people see the word "training", they think only of potties – it would be a pity to disappoint anyone and omit this aspect altogether.

Potty training is one of those subjects which looms very large with the first or even the second child, but which ceases to be important after that. The reason for this is that you discover, after just a couple of runs-through, that your child will eventually master the technique of bladder and bowel control, even if at times it seems as though he never will. You also realise that the best contribution you can make towards ensuring this mastery is not to worry about it.

I feel sure that it is often the parents worrying too much about toileting in the first place that produces many of the problems, because it makes the activity seem very "special" and fraught to the child.

Of course, children do not understand that your concern to get them potty-trained is because you want to avoid the mess and bother of the untrained state. Their daily motion probably looks just as satisfactory to them decorating the carpet or strategically placed in a doorway, and they cannot understand what all the fuss is about when they do it.

Then they get their mother kneeling next to them when they are on their potty – in fact trying to keep them on it for long enough for them to do something. The furrowed brow, the clasped hands, the concern being registered – what are they supposed to do? Children always like to interact with their parents, and it is their natural instinct to do so. Because they do not understand what it is their mother wants or, if they do understand, are not able to produce it at will, they will be quite likely to produce symptoms of distress, rage, hysteria or anything else which they think might be appropriate at the time.

Naturally enough, this causes the mother to be even more worried because this is tangible evidence of some very great problem. If she is not very careful she will be driven to consult some of the crazy theories that have been dreamed up by experts, wrestling with the problem at a distance.

For some reason it does appear that there are rather more bizarre explanations of children's behaviour in this respect than almost any other; possibly because, in childcare terms, it is on the sensational side – as are some of the theories!

It has even been suggested that one way of making the child enjoy using his pot is to allow him to make free with whatever he does in it, perhaps painting and decorating a specially prepared wall! Gosh! That would be fun wouldn't it? One can just imagine it with the postman at the door, another baby waiting to be fed or everyone sitting down to dinner.

On the whole, it is probably better if the mother just addresses herself to the simple problem itself, unencumbered by helpful theories. That is – how do you get a child to use a potty regularly and without fuss? The most useful piece of equipment to help with potty training is the potty chair.

A typical old-fashioned potty-chair is just a little straight-legged chair, either high or low, with a tray in front and a potty underneath a lift-up seat. Because of the support of the tray in front, a child can sit in it from about eight months or so and will start to do a number of his daily motions in it from the beginning. This is not because he knows what it is for, but simply because when you take his nappy off, sit him down and put something on the tray to distract him such as his food or a toy, he relaxes and will then do whatever he has been holding back.

Some children will very quickly learn that this is a more pleasant way of doing things and within a couple of months will be clean at least during the day. Other children will go on like this doing perhaps one or two motions in the pot and the rest in their nappies for considerably more than another year.

But at least it is a help to get some of the day's business in the pot, and it does confine the process to a set time. Furthermore, you know that they are slowly bringing these particular bodily functions under their control.

There are several advantages to this method of potty-training, one of which is that it is as regular as mealtimes. Also it avoids the dramas that become associated with the function when you have to get a child to sit on a potty for no other reason than you want him to perform. Sheer boredom plays a large part in the resistance many children put up to this activity being performed three or four times a day. And who can blame them? They may also be very delighted and intrigued by what they have produced when they get off the pot and peer into it with some surprise. True they may even stretch out a hand towards it as if they are about to decorate some specially prepared wall! However, let me hastily assure you that such progressive behaviour can easily be avoided by the exercise of a considerable physical feat which involves conveying in one facial expression three contradictory emotions.

You must manage to look delighted at what he has done, disgusted at what it is and congratulatory of his efforts. You do this by screwing up your face as at a nasty smell, smiling all the time through the grimace and crowing with delight at the achievement whilst whisking it away.

Children do have a fascination with their bodily functions at this age, obviously because they are new and do not happen all the time, so they are often surprised by them. They have an almost impersonal approach to certain things which is reflected in the surprise they register when they look into their potty, and they laugh with delight and amusement when they break wind or burp.

Nor is it only the toilet functions that produce this detachment. I remember calling one of my children to have his nose wiped when small and his saying "It's all right. It's gone back inside now!" And the youngest, Oliver, coming in with a cut on his leg and saying "Look, Mama, I'm coming out!"

They do not see these processes as being quite part of themselves since they do not seem to have any control over them. It takes some children a time to realise that their more infrequent functions are also a part of themselves and that they can control them.

If the child has still not worked out how to use the potty regularly by the time he is, say, two and a half, you may find that the introduction of a very regular routine will help. That is, you bring him to his potty for a few minutes dead on every hour, regardless of whether he does anything or not. The repetition of this routine so many times a day will give even the slowest child a chance to understand what it is you want him to do. Your excessive pleasure when he succeeds and your disappointment when he does not, reinforces the lesson for him.

It is much more difficult for any child to be dry at night because of the length of time involved. A child who is not all that confident about bladder control during the day may well be having "accidents" until well past his fifth birthday or even later. With a child like this, putting him on a pot last thing at night will help but will not necessarily solve the problem.

You will just have to make some simple preparations whereby the inconvenience to yourself is minimised so that you do not become too fraught at the situation. If you have a waterproof mattress cover and three or four very light, fitted sheets always to hand, it will be a simple matter to change the bed if it has been watered again.

Then if you do the rounds last thing at night and find that the bed has suffered, you will not be so inclined to get upset because of the work it causes you.

It can all become a bit of a nightmare to a child if his unfortunate lapses cause commotion and worry when he is already bleary with sleep. Unfortunately, if I am anything to go by, one is not quite at one's best in terms of patience and diplomacy last thing at night, so it is just as well to make preparations earlier in the day for what may turn out to be another bad night.

Having the replacement sheets nearby, it becomes an easy matter to render the bed comfortable again with such incoherent and non-acrimonious mutterings as, "Poor old bed – wet again. Have to get him dry or he'll never be able to sleep!" If anything, the child will be inclined then to sympathise with the bed and not to feel that any real censure is directed at him.

One of the problems for children at this age is that they are often so conscious of their own failings with respect to bladder control at night that they even dream they are sitting on a toilet and are really distressed when they wake up, yet again, in the familiar warm pool.

Their lapses can therefore be blamed on caring too much about it rather than too little, which is why it is worth taking all the steps possible to ensure that you can remain cheerful and unconcerned at what is a very trying situation when you are tired. Even if the child wets the bed so regularly that you need to put a disposable nappy on him at night, it is still better to do it in a spirit of cheerful nonchalance that will not convey any sense of anxiety to the child.

There will come a time when the combination of cutting down liquids to a minimum at teatime and potting them last thing at night will start to have an effect. One day, you can depend upon it, they will be home – and dry.

The dynamics of spoiling

Some years ago, I remember reading about a survey carried out in the United States on children who were described as having been "progressively" reared. What was meant by this term was that they had been brought up more or less to have and to do what they wanted in childhood.

It was noted that a disproportionate number of children who had been brought up in this way tended to be more conformist and submissive in their attitudes and ways of life, than one would have expected given the unusual nature of their early training. Their parents had no doubt thought that they were making them independent and strong-minded by allowing them to do as they liked, but the survey concluded that the children's "capacity to protest" had never been sufficiently developed by parental opposition to their wishes during their formative years.

I mention this rather obscure and half-forgotten reference because it seems to me to give dimension to a phenomenon that one can detect in spoilt children – which is what I would call them – and that is that they feel unrealistically important in their own homes and sadly at a loss when they are out of them.

This "capacity to protest" at the discipline of others is a natural process of growing up which keeps pace with the perceptions and needs of the child. He grows up first in a world which is circumscribed by arbitrary rules, such as the fact that hot things burn and that if you are not careful you fall down stairs rather than up them. I do not believe that, to a young child, having to talk, eat or behave in a certain way is any more surprising or irksome than this. They accept discipline as easily as they accept the physical rules of the world into which they are born.

This is no doubt the reason why most societies throughout the ages have not made much of a song and dance about handing on the disciplines that are required by the way of life of the group. They are imposed easily and naturally by parents who usually have more pressing things to consider, such as the provision of food, shelter and protection for their families.

The absence of any discipline in childhood produces what is popularly called a "spoilt" child. This is an interesting choice of word and causes one to wonder where it derives from and how it came to be applied to children.

The *Oxford English Dictionary* gives the definition as "Spoilt: injured in character by excessive indulgence, lenience or deference". The source of the word goes back to the sixteenth century when it was used in the sense of affecting injuriously, especially to an irretrievable extent. Thus it would appear that the word has lost little of its earlier meaning and has changed little in its use, especially with regard to children.

One very seldom meets a spoilt child who is cheerful, outgoing and generous. Left to follow his own desires or inclinations he becomes querulous and bad-tempered at not knowing where the limits are. He neither gives pleasure nor, more significantly, seems to derive any himself from what he has. There seems to be something in the very nature of trying to give a child everything he thinks he wants that is doomed to fail as a means of making him either happy or pleasant. Instead of being full of largesse as a result of his good fortune, he is jealous and mean with his things, disliking to give them away or share them, even to please friends.

Such a child derives little pleasure from his possessions or his power, which is a real object lesson on the effect of spoiling. The very hallmark of the spoilt child is that he is discontent, and that should tell you, if nothing else does, that parents who spoil their children are doing it – whether they realise it or not – primarily for their own sakes.

It seems to me that there are no two ways about it. If you want your child to grow up to be a person who will be concerned for other people, and who will be prepared to be co-operative rather than entirely selfish, then you have to bring him up that way from the outset. The very first step in this process is teaching the child that he cannot have everything he sees and he cannot do everything he wants.

It does not take a lot of experience before you realise that to defer always to a child's wishes is not the best way to prepare him for the give and take of ordinary life – rather it puts him at a disadvantage. It gives him a false sense of his own importance in his early years which all subsequent experience will show him was unrealistic. Poor little wretch; his early years will be a succession of shocks, starting with school, when he realises that everyone is not like mummy and is not going to play the game according to his rules. It is enough to give any child a permanent chip on his shoulder – which is exactly what many of them develop.

Nor is it at all *kind* of parents to allow their child to grow up with an inconsiderate and rude attitude towards others, and the belief that they are only there to serve and please him with no feelings of their own to be taken into account.

It may be a weakness of human nature, but children as much as adults value and appreciate things which have to be worked for, and are more careless of things they have acquired automatically or without much effort. They are critical and dismissive of teachers at school who are too lenient and seldom have an interest in anything they teach. Even parents who have been too pliant and indulgent often suffer from an openly disgruntled and contemptuous attitude from their child as a reward for having made no demands on them.

It is hardly a child's fault if he is allowed to develop in this way, without respect for the desires of others or regard for their feelings – but it is he who will have to pay the price for it. How many times has one seen a badly-behaved child running riot in some situation or other, and felt the anger and disapproval of the people around. Many adults are inclined to be rather inhibited in their behaviour towards children at the best of times, but on occasions like this the tight lips and cold stares speak volumes. So do the steely glances full of dislike directed at the child when the mother is not looking which would wither even an adult where he stood!

On the whole, children are very sensitive and are well used to picking up non-verbal expression of emotions. After all, it has been their primary means of communication for a long time and so this feeling of dislike and disapproval communicates itself to them very clearly and must have a corresponding effect upon their own good spirits and confidence. They sense the rejection, and this causes them to turn away from people and run back to Mummy with their resentment and confusion. This perhaps explains why so many very spoiled children are so clingy to their mothers and unwilling to go to others. Their mother has helped to cut them off from other people by the behaviour she tolerates.

Indulging

One does notice, however, that when parents refers to a child other than their own as "spoilt", they usually mean it in the sense of "irretrievably injured". Whereas, by means of the gentle alchemy which turns our own faults into approximate virtues, when they refer to their own child as "spoilt" they usually mean that he is more or less indulged.

There is, too, a difference between the concepts implied by the two words, because an *indulged* child is not necessarily an undisciplined one, but a *spoilt* child is. If you lead the kind of comfortable life which means help in the house and fewer chores for everybody, plenty of good food and enjoyable outings, it is only natural that the child is part of the same pattern. You cannot, after all, exclude him and nor would it be sensible to do so.

What matters is not what they receive but whether they are thoughtful and generous with what they have, and mindful of others who either have less or who have needs of other kinds. It is important for them to realise that poverty is not the only ill that people can suffer from, and that money is not the answer to everything. There are always old, lonely or incapacitated people about – even within a family group – and a smile, a visit or a genuine display of interest goes further with them than any amount of money or material things. In other words, generosity does not mean money alone – it means time, sympathy and effort also.

Probably the greatest risk that you run when you indulge a child too much is that you will make him too dependent upon material comforts and a pleasant, easy life. This can place a limitation on his movements and activities since he may find it hard to do anything – however enjoyable – where comfort is not of a high order.

One of my brothers took an assortment of our respective children walking around Hadrian's Wall for a few days at Easter. A friend went with them whose mother deposited him at our house complete with pyjamas, radio, airbed and tins and tins of his favourite food. He had to leave them all behind since no-one was prepared to help him carry them and, though he eventually enjoyed the trip, he spoke of it afterwards rather in terms of a foray with the Foreign Legion where his manhood had been severely tested, and he was not anxious to repeat the experience.

The other danger inherent in having a good standard of living is that it can become the means by which a child is robbed of taking pleasure in things. One has to remind oneself that pleasure is what one feels and is not what one is given; that it is only a feeling and not an object. Now that might sound perfectly obvious to most people, and yet how often, in practice, do we act as if it were not so.

Consider the subject of children's toys, for example. It must be many people's experience that the first baby is the one which attracts all the presents. Clothes, equipment and fluffy toys appear from friends and family who are rejoicing that you have decided to do something settled at last – and, of course, it means nothing to the baby but a lot to the happy parents.

Amongst the initial gifts that I received for Emma, our first child, were no less than five teddy bears which we put all round her cradle. She showed a mild interest in them at times, and would occasionally throw them about, but she never really played with any of them.

Then, for her first birthday, a little girl knitted her a teddy that was a real beast. It was dark green like a poison bottle with red eyes reminiscent of *The Hound of the Baskervilles*. Its arms were of unequal length and one ear hung over its face giving it a drunken, debauched air.

For Emma it was love at first sight and she took it to her bosom like a long-lost friend. They were inseparable from the first, and she shared all her pleasures and tribulations with it for many years afterwards.

To me it was the first lesson in the dynamics of pleasure for a child, that all subsequent experience has confirmed. The reason she enjoyed the special teddy so much was because it was the only *special* one and she could relate to it. It was a possession on a small scale which she could cope with without effort. It is very possible to swamp a child's capacity to enjoy things by giving him too much and, in the end, this decreases pleasure rather than adds to it.

It really is true that, in general, five teddies given to a child rather than one means less pleasure and not more, and that several special presents given together halves the enjoyment that would have been derived from only one.

I put away the redundant teddies, and, since they were all what the adverts coyly call "nearly new", they were given out, one by one, to all the new additions. In fact they lasted nicely, with Oliver arriving just in time to save the last doleful Koala from succumbing to moth or mould.

I always kept a large paper bag at the top of a cupboard which was full of toys that were acquired or given at times when they would have been just another possession for the child. I would give them out only at Christmas or birthdays, or when spirits were flagging and a little boost was needed to gladden the heart.

We often used to recall at home a boy who came into our shop when we lived out in the country. As well as selling my husband's prints and paintings, we sold craft work and toys made by people in the village and in little workshops all over East Anglia. We had an amazing collection of fascinating and ingenious things, and it was a real Aladdin's cave to us, full of interest and possibilities. One Saturday a lady came in with this gloomy and sullen boy whose twelfth birthday it was. They had spent the whole morning touring the area trying to find him something he wanted and they had drawn a complete blank.

"Na, Na", was all he said as the children showed him all the things they thought were really good, until they began to question him with some indignation as to what he *did* like. "Nothing", he said. "That's the trouble", his mother trilled complacently, "he's got everything!"

And indeed, he did have. There was nothing we could mention, from a portable colour TV for his bedroom to a pony, clothes, games, animals and toys that he had not already been surfeited with. I finally suggested she buy him a cobra and left it at that, and he wandered out with his mother still trying to animate his long-dead desires.

The children were incredulous and appalled. "That *poor* boy" they said, "fancy not wanting *anything!*" For them it must have been like seeing someone living without ambition and without hope.

Greed

I remember years ago being very impressed by that part of the end of Tolstoy's *War and Peace* where dear Nicholas Rostov, learning to appreciate his wife's character more and more after years of marriage, and wanting to know more of her inner thoughts, reads her diary. He begs her pardon for his curiosity and says how impressed he was by her account of how he had punished one of their children for greediness by making him go without pudding. She had observed that the look of greed on the child's face as he watched the others eating was quite sufficient to demonstrate that, as a punishment designed to deter greed, it was counter-productive.

This kind of ruminating about children with people who have a lot of their own is fascinating – and Tolstoy had thirteen. There are traits and tendencies in children which can be either modified or intensified by how you respond to them when the child is too young to want to disguise them from himself or anyone else. What is so endlessly interesting about spending a lot of time with children is that you gradually discover those things which you can influence, and which are the areas where their own innate tendencies or inclinations are too intrinsic for you to alter.

It is fairly safe to say that you cannot give a child a talent for something where none exists, although you can make them passable practitioners at almost anything.

Likewise, you cannot increase very dramatically the scale upon which a child thinks even though you can widen his horizon considerably by what you make available to stimulate thought. If they are not very interested in ideas or in making imaginative leaps themselves, children will follow quite happily and with interest what other people may do in that respect but, left to themselves will produce always what is within keeping of their true scope. "As the twig is bent, so the tree will grow", says the old proverb, and one has to accept it.

But behaviour is another matter entirely, and I would like to return to the problem of dealing with greediness. On first reading the episode from *War and Peace* referred to above, I concluded that Tolstoy was advocating curing the fault by satisfying the appetite that gave rise to it. In time I came to realise that he was, in fact, probably making the same point as Dr Johnson made in an anecdote related by Boswell. Upon being told that an acquaintance had sent his son to public school in order to cure him of excessive timidity, he remarked, "It is a preposterous expedient for removing his infirmity; such a disposition should be cultivated in the shade. Placing him at public school is forcing an owl upon day".

This is a true observation about certain kinds of faults that are yet not quite deliberate but are more predispositions. They need more subtle means than punishment to discourage or redirect them. However, these were early days as a parent and I decided to tackle the vexed question of my children's sweet-eating habits armed with the same principle.

We had three little children at the time, the oldest of whom was five, and we had hoped to do without sweets for most of the time because they were bad for the teeth and diet and they were expensive.

However, everyone seemed to take this abstemiousness on our part as a sign of the kind of pitiful poverty that they could do something about. Even normally vulpine shopkeepers would give the children sweets for nothing when I said I was not going to buy them any, and friends and neighbours were even worse. What can one do when an elderly relative comes tottering in at the door, weighed down with bags containing boiled sweets and rock that they have bought with what was left over from their pension every week? You find yourself unable to produce the brisk arguments which would limit what was being unloaded onto your gleeful infants and you just succumb.

In consequence, of course, they all developed voracious appetites for sticky sweets and chocolates and it became quite a struggle each and every time we went into, or even near, a shop with a sweet counter.

At last I decided to cure the obsession by satisfying it as far as was possible and so I bought pounds of sweets and chocolates – oh, the pain – and gave them out in handfuls whenever they wanted them.

To my amazement, they always did! They would say, "How many can we have?" and I would reply, "As many as you like", with an air of breezy unconcern – and the next time I looked they would have swiped the lot and would be busy salting them away in pockets, bags or secret boxes.

It will pass, I thought, and they will get used to the idea and then bored with sweets, but they did not. After several weeks of this ludicrous experiment they were still eating a tremendous number of sweets and, because of it, less of everything else. They had not stopped quarrelling over who had most and they hoarded them like mad; never bringing them out spontaneously when anyone called and never leaving them around where someone else could pick them up.

So, without any more ado, we reverted to a system which had operated in my own home as a child, and to which I had never given a second thought before. That was of having a sweet ration, which was received only at the weekend and which was called the "Saturday Special". Any sweets received during the week, from whatever source, were saved and added to the pile for the end of the week.

Once the system was imposed, by a neat *volte-face* that a mother who is good at carrying her audience can always achieve without fuss, the advantages were enormous.

The most practical benefit was that the children and their teeth were much healthier. Despite never having been the most assiduous of teeth-cleaners, all of my children have healthy, cavity-free teeth, and their dentist swears that it is because they are unaffected by sweets for most of the time.

The second advantage is aesthetic and equally important. They really did look forward to their "Saturday Special" and still regarded it as a treat even after many years. They would automatically put in the drawer any confectionery that they were given during the week and would often tell one another not to "spoil" the feast by indulging themselves in between times.

The "Saturday Special" itself is what a good food guide would describe as "wretchedly small": a tube of smarties, a sherbet dab, a few boiled sweets and a handful of toffees. Sometimes, when I was putting out the six little piles after lunch on a Saturday, my husband would observe that I should have been catering officer at Dotheboys Hall! But the children thought it was a feast and they could make it last for hours.

They played games using them as both counters and winnings; they swapped them with the other children because it was a special occasion and they felt expansive and generous.

Actually, if you think about it, adults behave in exactly the same way. People in pubs or at parties or dances are always more receptive to raffle tickets or collecting tins being passed round because the jolly occasion makes them forget how important money is to them normally!

Really the last thing to say on this subject is that allowing your children to derive the maximum enjoyment from small things is to teach them a valuable lesson for life.

The whole point of treats of whatever kind is that they provide a focus for enjoyment and an occasion to celebrate. Without them, all sorts of things which are intended to make life more enjoyable and to vary the daily routine become completely commonplace and so fail to affect us in any way. In the end there can be no greater deprivation you can inflict upon a child than to make interesting and pleasurable things habitually boring.

Such a state of mind must lead, at least in some cases, to the situation where young people turn for excitement and stimulus to dangerous or even criminal pastimes, and all the pathless woes that these can lead to.

A tighter grip on the family purse – however stuffed it may be – will help children to cultivate those pleasant and genuinely social qualities which they may otherwise find difficult to acquire. In particular, it will help to nurture what G K Chesterton described as "the highest form of thought" – gratitude.

Discipline

Having talked about spoiling, we move on to its antidote, discipline, and the role it plays in streamlining a child's emotions and placing the reins of responsible self-management firmly in his hands.

There are many and various kinds of discipline, and the need for them accompanies us through life but, with children, one important but commonplace aspect is considered controversial, and that is when it involves anything physical.

So I propose to plunge in right away and say what ninety-five percent of parents know by instinct and experience, but may not have the confidence to assert in the face of modish liberal opinion: that smacking is an essential part of bringing up a child.

That is not to say how much it should be done, or how little; or even that every child will need it – although most do. It is just that there will be times when there is no good substitute for it that is as quick, effective and, yes, beneficial. We do say a "good smack" because common vocabulary is always truthful, revealing and based on experience. This is, no doubt, why people who want to distort our perception of reality – like dictators and social engineers – always want to get their hands on it.

The problem is that smacking children moderately is a question of common sense and, by definition, it never really needs to be analysed because it is a widely shared thing. Indeed, the philosopher Thomas Aquinas observed in the thirteenth century that common sense *is* reality and, though most people cannot define it, they will always recognise it.

Therefore, when a person who is well qualified in medicine, psychology or the law confidently announces they have new "evidence" which flatly contradicts some common-sense proposition, it is extremely difficult for ordinary people to answer them effectively. We do not question our common-sense practices because they work well, and so we do not need to. If they didn't work, of course, people would have abandoned them long ago rather than continuing them until they became a tradition.

A tradition implies a test; the experience is tested, not a hundred times, or even a thousand – but millions of times by ordinary people as they go about their daily lives. If the tradition works for them too, then it takes its place amongst what Aquinas called "the dumb certainties of experience".

Now, in the matter of smacking children, I would guess that most of the parents who ever lived would agree with me that it is natural and necessary. However, a number of childcare professionals have become very disapproving of it over the last few years and feel, because it is physical, that it is uniquely damaging and dangerous. In this concern they are probably only reflecting a more general disquiet at the disturbing increase in all forms of violence, including within the family. They want to make smacking illegal since, they say, it legitimises violence and leads on to serious physical abuse.

The greatest flaw in their argument is, of course, that parents have always smacked their children and so that fact alone cannot possibly account for any sudden increase in violence.

In any case, it seems strangely blind that they should ignore the effect of a genuinely new influence on peoples' lives that *has* coincided neatly with this increase in violence and cruelty. That is the effect of a media culture that depends upon shock and brutality to an unprecedented extent. It is an old observation that "there is a pathway from the eyes to the emotions which completely bypasses the brain", which is likely to be far more relevant to the problem of violence in our society.

However, this argument about the necessity of smacking at times is one that parents must meet head on and repudiate with confidence if they are to avoid, later on, the inescapable parallel logic of being told that they must not kiss or cuddle their children because that can lead to sexual abuse. Common sense tells us in all these things where to draw the line, and most people are perfectly capable of judging where that line is. Indeed, if they were not, there would be no sense in urging people to go in for alternative forms of punishment such as emotional ones, since people would be no more capable of knowing where to draw the line there either.

What some people ignore or forget is that the alternative to smacking a child is not, in most cases, the use of sweet reason. Though it is easy to claim, in a discussion, that calmly talking to a badly behaved child is the only acceptable way to impose discipline – the reality is that the person doing the "talking to" is likely to be an angry and frustrated adult. Angry words and insults – not to mention what American psychologists call "belittling character assassination" is likely to be far more evident than sweet, loving reason. It does not surprise me in the least that, as you will see from Appendix One in this book, that research in America has discovered that children remember things said to them in anger for far longer than they ever remember a routine smack.

In fact, fashionable, professional opinion is far more likely to go to absurd extremes in both physical and emotional punishments than traditional opinion ever has. It was, after all, only a hundred years ago that experts in the childcare field believed in whipping and flogging children for the slightest offence and locking them in solitary confinement for hours and even days on end. Now they have flown to the other extreme, leaving parents and the domestic tradition more or less where they always were, on the moderate middle ground.

In case you think I am exaggerating in saying expert opinion could easily turn against parental affection next, let me quote from a famous and influential child psychologist, John B Watson. In a very peculiar book written in 1928, *Psychological Care of Infant and Child,* he offered this authoritative advice on caring for our infants: "Never hug and kiss them, never let them sit on your lap. If you must, kiss them once on the forehead when they say goodnight. Shake hands with them in the morning". He also said that "Mother love is a dangerous instrument" that could wreck a child's chance of happiness. As a result of this absurd advice, more than a generation of children whose parents were persuaded to follow it were deprived of the comfort and emotional education of a loving, physical relationship in their early years. One wonders how many of today's emotional casualties are not directly attributable to the loveless childhood once advocated by this discredited expert.

In view of how barbarous and damaging this advice now seems to us, one might well ask how on earth professionals can be so wrong in their assessment of what children need for their development. Don't they spend all their time working with children and studying them?

Perhaps that is a question for professionals themselves to answer. The rest of us can only note that, for upwards of thirty years, doctors and psychologists would only allow parents very limited access to their sick children in hospital on the grounds that their presence upset the children. What is more, until the late 1960s they opposed the use of foster parents for even babies in care, preferring to use residential institutions.

This horrible practice was only brought to an end by the decisive influence of a psychoanalyst, James Robertson, who filmed a little boy going to pieces over a nine-day period in an institution. That shows that the catastrophic effects on the children were obvious at least to the camera, if not to the various professionals actually looking after them. The film met with great hostility from the medical and psychological professions although they did, eventually, close their residential nurseries.

So, for the benefit of any parents who feel under threat from today's professional childcare experts in the matter of smacking, I should like to set out the common sense of the practice.

Firstly, it is for simple *correction* that is quick, minimally painful both physically and emotionally and, before the age of reason, easily understood by the child. It supplies the basic model of all correction in human affairs; that impulsive, anti-social behaviour is restrained by fear of the consequences. The point is that the child *learns* what it must and must not do by these early means and, once it has learnt, the corrected behaviour remains and the need for the sanction gradually disappears.

Secondly, and most importantly, it is the means by which a child's aggressive instincts are trained. These instincts are perfectly natural and, indeed, necessary for personal and collective survival, although they vary from child to child. As they get older, of course, they generally become far stronger and more destructive in boys, but in both sexes they need to be trained as early as possible if they are not to become purely self-serving.

This training is mostly undertaken in the early years by the mother who is the ideal person to do it since she combines love and concern for the child with a physical presence that is not too intimidating in the way that a man's deep voice and physical power is. She needs, at this time, to demonstrate clear limits to the pleasure and power of these aggressive feelings.

It is no good pretending they are not there or that they will go away if you ignore them; they need to be out in the open if they are to be educated; and our collective, domestic experience has obviously found these feelings and impulses to be unresponsive, or even impervious, to reasoning. This really should not surprise us since, very often in life, we see that sound reason alone does not have the power either to encourage us into, or deter us from certain actions.

Just think for a moment, of what it would be like for a toddler to try to learn to walk if it could not feel pain. When you watch those first brave steps into equilibrium, you flinch a thousand times for the near-misses which accompany their efforts; the split second movement of the head to avoid the edge of a table, the careful precision that replaces the blundering early movements. The bumps and grazes of their early attempts at finding their feet are nature's painful input into this learning process. You can see then what a "gift of nature" pain is. It educates the brain, not with reason but with non-rancorous, impersonal sensation – and a child is programmed to respond to it. It is not an exaggeration to say that a child would be a danger to himself if he could not feel pain. It is also impossible to imagine how one could substitute warnings and admonitions to replace that vital effect.

I believe that parents have always used this natural model when it came to instructing their children in acceptable behaviour. After all, in many societies in the past, including our own, what would be considered merely delinquent behaviour today, would have resulted in them being transported abroad or even hanged. In other words, good behaviour was as crucial to their survival then, as muscular control and prudence were to their physical safety.

It is mere sentimentality to blackguard this natural phenomenon as something too cruel for childhood and to seek to prevent parents building upon it – judiciously and with love. As a matter of fact, pain warns and protects us all our lives. I remember a doctor explaining on the radio, that lepers suffer terrible injuries and lose their fingers and toes to gangrene, because they can not feel pain. The disease makes their extremities insensitive to pain and it is this which makes the patients injure themselves through carelessness.

In smacking a child for aggressive or defiant behaviour a mother is demonstrating a central fact of life; that there are two kinds of violence and the difference between them is crucial. Put simply, there is the sort that refuses to stop kicking the cat for fun and the sort that defends the cat from attack. In human affairs, one could say that there would be no point in shouting for "Help!" when attacked, if we didn't have an absolute faith that there was another kind of violence that could "help" us.

Ordinary parental "violence" is legitimate because it is measured and has a moral intention. When physical correction is used at an early age, therefore, it instils the lesson that the capacity for violence which is always with us, must have the same moderation and moral purpose.

Children understand this intuitively and accept it without resentment provided it is not excessive, which is no doubt why the vast majority of them grow up to be well-adjusted and law-abiding.

It also explains the phenomenon that rightly worries childcare professionals; the violent child who comes from a home where random violence is commonplace. Such children have never learnt the difference between legitimate and illegitimate violence and their aggressive instincts run riot.

In the same way it explains the contrary condition which is even more common today where the child is *never* smacked and yet is spiteful and aggressive. They too have not had their aggressive instincts effectively educated.

It has often seemed to me that this technique of administering a mild dose of physical correction as a means of curbing potentially much larger manifestations of aggression is essentially the same principle as vaccination or even homeopathic medicine. It is very strange, but nonetheless true, that in both of these a small, non-lethal dose of the same thing is the key to a cure.

However, in case anyone should misunderstand me, let me make it clear that "using physical means" does not mean bullying children nor does it mean slapping them about merely because you happen to be in a bad mood. We are not even talking about "hitting" children because that word has other connotations of ill-intentioned violence which do not belong in the relationship between parent and child. What it does mean is that there will be times when bad behaviour is more appropriately met by a physical response than anything else because it is quick, educative, and doesn't waste anyone's time.

My mother always used to say that smacking was useful for the things which did not matter very much. For the more serious things that children do wrong like habitual lying, stealing or nastiness, a good talking to, in order to discover what is really going on, is likely to be the only effective method of correction. Then you can make the child understand the situation himself and animate his *imagination* so that he sees what he is doing and feels for the people he is injuring.

I have already distinguished between smacking and the violence of "hitting" by the intention as well as by the degree of force used. Of course the *degree* of force is crucial, as it is in most things in life, and we may have to learn how to smack sensibly just as we have to acquire other skills of degree when dealing with children: how to give a baby food at the right temperature or a bath that will not scald, for example.

One quite frequently comes across parents who are not used to smacking their children and who, when driven to it by sheer exasperation, will do it far too hard. Whether it is because of guilt or embarrassment I do not know, but there are many occasions when one winces at a clumsy blow bestowed by a normally over-indulgent parent.

It reminds me of the year I spent doing various "au pair" jobs in France before going to university. In one family there were several little girls to whom I had to teach English and for whom I was a sort of old-fashioned "nanny". Their parents were rather progressive in their outlook but had very little to do with the daily management of their children since they had a full complement of staff to do the job. I was thus rather disconcerted to discover that it was considered my responsibility to contend with the kind of wildness that their lack of involvement could tolerate with ease.

Sometimes during the late afternoon the children would join their parents in the drawing-room and, on one such occasion, the mother was going over a piece of homework that one of the girls had done badly.

Mother was unused to her daughter's bad manners and truculence and it clearly enraged her that she could not get any co-operation or effort from her. They had a subdued but acrimonious conversation and later, when we returned to the nursery, I discovered on the little girl's arm, three deep, crescent-shaped cuts where her mother's finger nails had sunk in as she "reasoned" with her child in a rage that was all the more excessive for being repressed.

To me it was a classic case of phoney kindliness breaking down under quite ordinary pressure and producing the kind of viciousness that cannot be excused. Had the children in this case been judiciously smacked more often in the recent past, they would not have been such little beasts, capable of arousing such ferocious reactions in a parent. It seems to me that there could be many occasions when parents who have not previously disciplined their children in any way are driven to fury by consistent bad behaviour until something in them snaps and they lash out in an uncontrolled manner that can seriously injure a child.

It would be much healthier if people felt able to be honest and admit without shame that smacking is something they do at one time or another. It is not exactly a secret vice and yet, in certain influential and professional circles, people treat it as if it were.

It gives rise to some painfully tortuous behaviour on the part of mothers in particular who feel obliged to try and live by such fantasies. A typical conversation I had on the subject recently went like this:

Kind Friend (worried): "James keeps throwing his food on the floor whenever he does not like something or has had enough. It makes such a mess and I clear it up and he does it again! What would you have done if one of yours did that?"

Me (cheerful): "Oh, I'd smack him and make him do without anything else till he cleared it up".

Friend (pensive): "Gosh! Really! (pause) I don't agree with using violence on children, of course; although I must admit that I *do* very occasionally smack him. But only when he's driven me absolutely mad and there's just nothing else I can do to keep *sane* or make him behave".

Now this is completely the wrong way round. From the parent's point of view, as long as they are feeling cheerful and able to cope, their child leads them a dog's life. From James' point of view, he gets clobbered every so often for something that cannot seem all that different from his normal behaviour.

How can he be expected to know where he stands? And how can parents feel proud of the fact that they are only effective when they are in a temper?

You are avoiding the reality of the situation if you seek to use only reason to limit the actions of a child whose physical expression is seeking a physical response. There is something desperately inappropriate in the rationalistic bleatings of a mother to a wild boy who is going through a stage when he is physically aggressive and wants to know what pain is.

"Oh, darling! You hit poor little Johnny. Yes you did, dear: we all saw you. You did it on purpose, too, didn't you? And he hadn't done anything to you, had he? That wasn't kind, was it? No it wasn't! You wouldn't like someone to do that to you, would you? What do you mean you'd like them to try? You jolly well wouldn't. Well, if you aren't going to say sorry, you can just go away. We don't like little boys who won't say sorry. And we'll give Johnny a chocolate too."

It is such a pointless form of nagging because the child knows perfectly well that he is in the wrong and being anti-social. That is why he did it in the first place! He is looking for opposition. He wants to run up against something muscular because he is unconsciously shadow-boxing with himself, trying to develop his own strength.

The nagging, however refined and constructive it gets, is no substitute for the physical effect that such a child needs at the time, and so it achieves nothing. The mother has bled her own response so white that it no longer has any life for him and neither party gets anything from such an exchange. On the contrary, the very aggression that the mother hoped to talk out of existence will be reinforced by resentment rather than diminished or re-routed.

In smacking a child for bad behaviour one is not simply using violence to quell violence as the fashionable viewpoint has it. What you are doing is showing him honestly the violent potential in both of you. You are together enacting a scene from the countless stories about "goodies" and "baddies" and you are the good guy who stops the bad one in his tracks. You are showing, by means of real drama, that you too have an ability to be violent that you use legitimately to curb wrong-doing.

The child will take the point and see the distinction perfectly. It helps him to educate his aggressive feelings rather than denying them or pretending that they can be wished away. He needs to recognise them for what they are – a part of himself that must be used only in conjunction with good reason.

This distinction between different kinds of violence is not just a subtle form of words with no relation to recognisable reality. It is as plain as a pikestaff and forms the basis for most of the best-loved stories and films about adventure for adults as well as children. It is the story of the good man using as much force, and more, than the bad, and triumphing because he is fortified by right.

The fact that nearly all children enjoy stories in which the good and the bad are in conflict indicates to me just how naturally they identify with and feel at home with physical solutions to certain situations. It satisfies their sense of justice and fitness, and no amount of teaching and propaganda has done anything to make them prefer mythical heroes who go around using non-physical means to subdue wrong-doers.

However, to start with young children and your relationship with them, it can be seen that, although in many respects it is a physical one, such disciplining as you do will not be of the "punishing" variety at all; it is simply *correction*. You will be teaching them by physical means and that is very different. Indeed, the fact that it is physical in the same way as kissing and cuddling, associates what is being taught with a loving relationship.

Let us take the case of a child of about a year old who has got to the very common stage where he is bored with having his nappy changed. He thrashes about with his legs, kicking the nappy off just when it is in position and heaving his bottom in the air so that you cannot get the nappy back on. This can develop into a battle between his will and your determination to do the job at every nappy change. You cannot reason with him; all you can do is to try and distract him, and if he spurns that you are sunk!

Instead of this time-wasting hassle, if you give him a good-humoured but purposeful little slap on the thigh and say "No", he will stop instantly and gaze at you in surprise. He will not cry because it won't hurt but he will look intently to see what it is all about. So you don't let much show on your face but perhaps twitch your eyebrows and hum distractedly whilst pressing on with the job.

He will start to wriggle again and you will slap again – just as he expected. You are communicating exact meaning to him and he knows it. Before many nappy-changes are passed, the task will be so far improved that he will do only a sample throwing about for you and you will give him a sample slap and he will be very satisfied with that. He is learning the basis of co-operation.

Similarly, when he is at the stage where he keeps grabbing for everything give him a firm tap on that acquisitive little paw. Not so that it hurts much – that is not the intention – but so that he *feels* it and knows what you mean. If you do it with the right amount of calm confidence and without any rancour, he will not even cry. You are teaching him in a physical way which is appropriate, effective and natural since everything in his world is expressed by such physical means.

One should not forget that pain is, in nature, the "warning shot" that alerts us to danger or damage. Taking notice of it must be written in our genes which is why it is a very impersonal teacher. Clumsy or inadequate movements and over-confident forays result in bumps and bruises from which a more circumspect and skilful approach to life develops.

A strong-minded toddler can take a good deal of exertion on your part to keep him in order and stop him from developing ways that are too aggressive, demanding and selfish. They are by now fully capable of kicking up a fuss if they do not get their own way and they can feel weakness in an adult just like a doctor feels for a fracture.

They can produce such a loud noise and such alarming displays of violence and temper that some parents capitulate completely. This *ensures* that, as a successful technique for getting their own way, it will be used, in various forms and disguises, throughout their lives.

Tantrums are just such displays of temper and the only way to deal with them in children is to quell them. They are very exhausting and upsetting and they waste so much of a child's time and energy that it is really not fair to allow him to become the victim of them.

For this reason, the most common alternative remedy – which is to just "walk away" and leave him to get on with it – is about the worst thing you can do. It may appear to mean that the mother can remain calm and uninvolved, but it is a foolish and unlikely pretence when her child is having the emotional equivalent of a fit! It prolongs the misery and waste for the child who must feel both resentment and despair that there is no-one who seems able to get him out of the mess.

Besides which, you may depend on it, if a child has been unable to punish you enough with his tantrum at home because you have just walked away, he will catch you with one later when escape is not so easy; like at the bus stop, on arrival at school, in a shop or in the library!

So what do you do? Well, the simplest way which usually works is to become absolutely indignant yourself and to completely overbear his tantrum with your righteous anger at it. You may have to pick him up off the floor since children usually cast themselves on the floor the better to scream and kick, and smack him about the legs with forceful and indignant cries. You have to be fairly loud yourself or else he won't hear you above his own din, and you must never be timid or apologetic about it.

You may have to exert yourself considerably in order to put on a display of indignation which is convincing enough to drive out his rage. But it is worth it for you both and, in a way, you owe it to your child.

He knows instantly when he cannot win, and that knowledge is a great relief to him. He needs to know your power because it is a deep source of security to him.

He already knows that you love him and so your strength is his strength and he trusts it. When the chips are down for him, it is to that strength that he turns for help, secure in the knowledge that it is greater than his own. He very quickly learns that tantrums are something which you simply will not allow and he will cease even to attempt them.

Children like to have their parents work with them on their emotions because it means that you are taking a keen interest in them and they enjoy that. They seem to get satisfaction too from the fact that they are being helped to cope with strong emotions. For them it must be like being pulled out of a bog by a firm, warm hand and they are very glad of it.

It is not a question of repressing emotions because the child will still have them but will learn, early on and before the feelings become outsize, how to control them. It so easily happens that children become victims of their strong, negative emotions instead of discovering that they are as much under their control as the rest of themselves – but they need to know it and they like to know it.

Incidentally, the security provided by a parental authority that is stronger than the child's own, is something that has wider implications. Not only is it superior to a child's own strength, it is also superior to the strength of those who might bully and intimidate the child outside the home. I have often wondered if the reason some children never tell their parents that they are being bullied at school is because they have never had a reasonable fear of their parents' authority themselves. They cannot seek its protection when they are threatened, because they are not in awe of it themselves. They don't trust their parents to control bullies because their parents cannot even control them!

However, in childhood, most of the things that children do wrong are not very serious and they only become so when they are wrongly handled and so aggravated until they become real problems.

Just what I mean by this can be illustrated by an example from the days when a friend and I ran a playgroup in our local village. A social worker referred to us a small boy of four who had been excluded from the social services nursery school for bad behaviour having been previously ejected from two other playgroups. They had been unable to "cope" with him and, as a last resort, the social worker hoped that we might be sufficiently different to give him a fresh start.

Someone came to see me with his "notes" which listed all the terrible things he had done. Glancing through them, they all seemed pretty ordinary to me; the sort of thing that any badly-behaved child might do if left to his own devices. But I supposed that it just might be possible that an incipient psychopath could cause fear and consternation amongst three or four perfectly healthy grown-ups!

When he turned up, however, with a mother who did a quick one-step out of the way as soon as she had left him, I recognised the type immediately. Bright red hair, stocky figure, knowing, bold eyes and a big voice. My own Irish relations are not so far distant that I do not have two or three of the same stamp, and I took to him right away. For his part, he set out right away to prove that his reputation for scaring all the ladies was not lightly based and he went to work with a will at creating disruption.

There were one or two minor skirmishes before he brought out his set piece for my appraisal which consisted of heaving himself up the climbing frame, dragging one of the tricycles behind him in order to bring it down on the heads of the children below. The repetition of this considerable feat when backs were turned at the nursery had sealed his fate there and he obviously hoped to dispose of us in the same way.

I watched him fascinated as he struggled and panted upwards with his "offensive weapon" and I noticed too how having grown-ups watching in no way inhibited him. He was not used to adults influencing his behaviour and he did not take them into account when deciding what he wanted to do. So absorbing was his behaviour that I was only just in time to catch the tricycle when he finally launched it with a hoarse and triumphant cry.

I lifted him off, sat down and put him across my knee, and gave him a couple of good smacks. He was furious; absolutely fighting mad at the unexpectedness of it and he flew at me trying to bite and kick. So I picked him up again and repeated the dose, explaining to him that there was no way he was going to win so he might as well behave himself.

He threw himself on the floor then, screaming at the top of his considerable voice and lashing about. So I dived in again, picked him up, put him across the by now familiar knee and raised my hot little hand – but it was over. He'd had enough!

"I'm not *going* to cry anymore", he said.

"Good", I said, "I don't like nasty boys and I *always* smack them. So you just behave yourself and we'll get on all right."

Now I realise at this point that I have to add something to my original text because various unrepresentative pressure groups have made this sort of response to a naughty child illegal, or at least frowned upon. The results are all around us with even primary schools subject to the violence and disruption of the naughty children. In some areas, curfews are imposed upon whole districts because no-one but "the authorities" are allowed to impose any form of discipline upon children. This crushing of adult rights to do what is necessary to maintain order in their families, schools and areas, has not been to the advantage of children. Indeed, they have been the first to suffer from the loss of order and calm in the classroom. It is to their disadvantage that good teachers have been driven out of the profession and that bullying has made many children afraid to go to school.

As for the naughty children themselves, their childish bad behaviour has been allowed to develop unchecked until they are at an age when they are a real problem to others. Then they are sent to spend their formative years with other "young offenders", where, of course, they learn to be even worse.

It's a mess and a scandal and I make no apology for describing in some detail the alternative, time-honoured way of dealing with that behaviour which now defeats us.

My little friend with the red hair would today be considered a child with "special needs". He would be analysed and examined and, by the time he was eleven, he would already be a marked man with a reputation to live up to. Quite likely, his prospects of a reasonable chance in life would be blighted by what he had been lead to believe were his "problems" and the turbulence of adolescence could only make things worse.

However, back in our old church-hall playschool, I promise you, that morning of decisive action was the first and last time "Rocky" as I called him, ever gave me any trouble. He was no better or worse than any of the other children, but he was reckless, brave and fiery. He loved a tussle and when I used to see him looking around with a sort of whooping delight for something physical to do I would call out, "OK son, go for your gun!" and he would launch himself at me in furious combat.

It was something that my eldest brother used to do regularly with the youngest one – there was ten years between them – and the secret of its success is for the bigger one to keep up a running commentary to the effect that the other one is almost winning. After mock wrestling on the floor with the small one clasped in your arms, you pretend he is on the point of overpowering you with his fearful strength!

"Ah, you nearly got me there, you brute; but I'm still king around here. I'm doing all right. Ouch, you nearly got me there too, but. . ." and so on. It's lovely and very tiring even for the big one, so what it is like for the toddler I cannot imagine. But they finish up flushed, happy and satisfied and quite exhausted.

Of course, I realise that there are occasions when this kind of activity with such a child just cannot be indulged in. Likewise there are a lot of women who would not consider doing anything so undignified and rough – which is, no doubt, where a lot of fathers come in. It just happened to suit me, but there are many alternatives along the same lines. Throwing balls about, dancing around, chasing, tickling madly or doing something physically tiring is what they want, where they can feel and enjoy your superiority whilst engaging with it. At such times they want to be genuinely challenged and not just amused and it gets rid of a lot of exuberance which, when it is disappointed, turns to aggression.

I never made any bones about smacking other people's children if they behaved badly because I think that it is not only very natural but it is far less harmful and debilitating than nagging, banishing a child from the social circle or "withdrawing approval", as some jargon would have it.

In fact, I never had to do it very much either to my own or to other people's children and the reason, I am sure, is that they knew they would be smacked if they did certain predictable things and so they did not do them. What is more, some notorious little brutes behaved themselves very well in our house because of it and so continued to be welcome with us, which was not always the case in more liberal establishments!

This has a direct parallel with schools at the moment. Just as badly behaved children are "excluded" from the homes of better-behaved children because no-one feels they have the right to be firm with them, so naughty children are excluded from school because teachers simply do not have the means to control them. The result of this supposedly "liberal" policy is that often the most needy children are "excluded" from the company of their peers and from all beneficial contact with education. If they were more decisively handled, many of them would certainly change their behaviour and eventually become worthwhile members of their school body.

There is no way that such a system can be passed off as a more enlightened approach to the problem of discipline than corporal punishment. It is certainly not more liberal to deprive a child of an education; to curfew whole areas; to electronically tag him like an animal, or – the latest wheeze – to fine the family by cutting off financial support if their child behaves badly. It seems that they will do anything rather than put the blame and the punishment, firmly where it belongs, onto the person of the delinquent teenager.

To add insult to injury, this illiberal policy of exclusion from school, and deprivation of liberty as a means of imposing discipline on children, has been spectacularly unsuccessful. But, since not even a worm in a puddle takes longer to die than an academic theory that has been espoused by politicians, we may have to wait a while yet until sanity returns.

In the meantime, you should never worry that you are going to crush the spirit out of your children because you impose discipline upon them. In the same way that children develop a sense of humour through laughing often and a habit of being loving through being loved – so they learn self-discipline through experiencing the discipline of others. It really is one of the satisfactions of rearing a family that as soon as children are old enough – and that age varies with individuals – they take over sensible disciplines for themselves and even extend them so that your role in their continuation ceases. Before you know it, they will be using it for their own ends; ordering and directing their lives with an acquired self-discipline that is a great source of satisfaction and confidence to them.

I might add that, on the other hand, insisting on excessive or ridiculous discipline in childhood is probably the quickest way to ensure that it is cast aside with a good deal of vigour as soon as the child is old enough to do so. Common sense is really the only guide here and, fortunately, both parent and children share it as often as not.

In the end, it is their own essential nature that will rise through all the extraneous discipline to assert itself in that confidence. The difference will be that, amongst all the other things, they will have learnt the kind of primary self-control that will mean you can discuss anything under the sun without anyone needing to fear that the subject will produce unbridled rudeness. abuse or estrangement.

It is so desperately important that young people pass into full independence with their parents' help and support to guide them and save them from many laborious mistakes, rather than being cut off from it because no one can talk about anything serious without the fur flying all over the place. Oscar Wilde remarked that children start by loving their parents; after a while they judge them; rarely, if ever, do they forgive them.

One cannot help feeling that if families keep alive the ability to talk about everything and anything, so that at least they understand each other properly, there will always be much to love and little to forgive.

It seems to me that children find only two things genuinely difficult to forgive. One is extremism of a destructive kind; being pushed into things well beyond their powers, being bullied rather than disciplined and indoctrinated rather than educated. They have an inherent sense of balance which draws them always towards the norm and causes them to react violently against extremes even when they are all the child has known.

The second is indifference on the part of their parents – the feeling that they are not very important, particularly to their mothers, has a demoralising effect on children which they recognise surprisingly early, and resent. Rightly or wrongly, the feeling of being important is closely related to the amount of time they are given – and never by the amount of things.

Many working women try to escape from this reality by referring to "quality time" spent with their children; by which they mean the small amount of playtime they give their children at the end of a day doing something else.

Unfortunately, as increasing numbers of women are discovering, children do not see it the same way and will subconsciously punish their mother for leaving them by displays of bad temper or difficult behaviour. There is just no getting away from it – in love affairs throughout life, love is expressed in *time*. The wonder is that children are born knowing it.

First impressions and early language

Learning in the broadest sense is something a child does from the moment he is born and possibly even earlier. More than one country midwife has said to me that "summer babies and winter babies are different" and the reason they gave for this was not astrological but practical.

In a cold birthroom, movements are hurried, confined and cursory with the main object being to get the baby wrapped up quickly to protect him from the cold. On a fine summer's day, the atmosphere is quite different. Warm hands receive the child in a more relaxed and leisurely fashion and there is likely to be more openness, laughter and the contentment that good weather brings.

If this is true – and I am quite prepared to believe it is – then it indicates that atmosphere is something even a very tiny baby absorbs and responds to in his own way. He is, in fact, *learning* something.

This perhaps explains why it is that the more children one has, the easier they become to handle. In my own immediate family we have between us twenty-three children, and when the three mothers responsible for this empire get together, we never talk about feeding or teething problems, crying or tummy upsets, because our later babies just do not have them.

Compared to the early children, the later ones cry less, sleep and feed better, appear very relaxed and accommodating and even suffer less from nappy rash. This last I find very difficult to understand since the nappy-changing routine did not alter very much except that, if anything, I was a less assiduous bottom-washer with the last than with the first – but he never had nappy-rash at all and neither did my sisters' children.

We long ago came to the conclusion that it is the spirit in which the babies are received that makes all the difference. You are not anxious about handling them and the various routines are second nature so they cause you no effort.

Uncertainty and tenseness communicates itself to children as it does to animals and they quickly take on the appropriate response which is to duplicate some of the qualities themselves. Conversely, the amiable mother, unconsciously doing what she now finds effortless, reassures and relaxes the baby in a way that makes other mothers think you must have drugged your child.

I remember watching, with dumb admiration, how the much-practised midwives who came daily after my two rural home confinements would change the nappy of the sleeping infant without waking him. Their assured and calm movements were so deft and yet gentle that not only was the child's rhythm of sleep unbroken, but also the lady could talk to me throughout.

In time I was able to do exactly the same myself, and sometimes would wonder how this harmony existed. It just seems to be a natural compensation for the extra work entailed in having many children – as you become more expert with practice, they respond by relaxing completely and become a pleasure to look after.

You are so used to having a baby "about your person", as you might say, that if he is snivelly or lonely you are quite able to write a letter or have a telephone conversation with him in your lap or lying next to you on the sofa with his feet against your leg.

Nor do you think the baby is in agony every time he cries, so when you hear a noise you do not parade your concern, but finish whatever you are doing before ambling over to give him some attention. In short, you accept him without fuss and he responds without fuss, which just shows that a lot of his learning is coming from you.

By the time he is three months old, the list of things he has learned will be impressive. He can get your attention with charming noises and whoops. He knows how to melt hearts and produce the most inane smiles on normally granite features by flashing a beaming, toothless smile. He knows exactly where on the horizon of his cradle you are likely to appear and the difference between strangers and friends of the house.

In the case of one's first child, being inexperienced, one does not realise how quickly they advance. It used to be the fashion to put babies face down to sleep. Whilst placing them on their sides does prevent them from choking if they are sick, they can still roll over onto their stomachs. Nowadays it is considered best to place them on their backs, as incidence of Sudden Infant Death Syndrome ("cot death") is reduced in this position.

For your part, during these early months, what really causes surprise is the extent to which the child has a will to do things. You have got so used to the idea of babies being passive creatures during the nine months of carrying them and the first few weeks of nursing them that it really catches you unawares to discover that they have a will and personality of their own that is struggling to be acknowledged.

You may be sitting alone in a room that is just as it used to be – except for the cradle in the corner – and feeling just as you used to at such times. Then suddenly you notice that this little scrap of humanity is actually craning his neck to look for you and that, far from being an inert object, he is watching your every move and devising – yes, devising – ways of getting your attention. They will go in for earnest babbling to hold your interest and try every one of their little tricks of the eyes and the smile to inveigle you into coming and playing with them.

It knocks you out to discover that they are as interested in you as you are in them without your having to do anything in particular to justify it. No day can ever be wholly bad when you have a baby because they are always so genuinely glad to see you and so happy in your company that it is wonderfully gratifying.

A relationship is beginning which will never end regardless of how temperamentally sympathetic or different you are. That inexhaustible interest in one another starts which is so much the prerogative of families and which has, as its several roots, a mutual interest in first movements, first steps, first sounds and words.

Early Language

The very earliest language of a child is quite simply confined to those few sounds that he is able to make. Thus "da-da" and "ma-ma" are universally the first words that a child says regardless of what the words for "father" and "mother" are in his native tongue. He uses them often because his parents encourage him to do so, identifying themselves with glad cries and constant repetition of the sounds.

From this the baby progresses to many more meaningless sounds until his parents provide him with another sound that he can repeat at will and associate with a meaning. My own children took to "taa" next because it enabled them to ask for things with it by pointing at an object and waggling their fingers with some urgency. After that came "nana" for banana and "din-din" which shows where their principal interest lay.

There is nothing surprising or unusual about any of this except for the fact that some parents seem to feel that they are wrong to use baby-talk and are ashamed to use it in front of other people. Perhaps they feel that they are talking down to a child and that this form of teaching makes them sound somehow not very enlightened.

Whatever the reason, it really is more important for the parents to realise that what they are doing is laying the foundations of a feeling for language. So-called "baby" words are full of unconscious poetic devices like alliteration, repetition and onomatopoeia (words that sound like what they describe: "splash", "gurgle", etc.) and, as such, are the tools that every person with a love of language uses. They make the use of language free and open to the imagination, which is why little children as well as poets like to use them.

The primary, but not the exclusive, aim of speech for babies is communication. They obviously derive considerable enjoyment from just making sounds, rather like a person singing; but they also want to communicate.

The first noises they make feel and sound pleasant to them, so it is upon this that you build, using the sounds as a basis for communicative words. If you aim too high in this respect and try to insist on the child saying words which are beyond his sound range, you will run the risk of making him less communicative, because accuracy will have become more important than expression or communication.

Just how dramatically you can inhibit a child's natural speech was clearly demonstrated a few years ago when we looked after a little boy of two who had only one word in his vocabulary, and that was "Mama". He was an only child and very bright. He could do many things that required skill and common sense, and he understood absolutely everything that was said to him.

Then we discovered with some hilarity that his mother would not allow him to use anything but the "right" word and was very strict about it. He had to say "father" and "thank you", "breakfast time" and "goodbye" if he was to remain uncorrected. In consequence he had simply clammed up rather than be told off all the time for his mistakes.

It was painful to watch the way in which, if he saw something that would cause an outburst of delight in a normal child – like a passing steam-roller, for example – he would look determinedly sideways and down at the floor as if cutting himself off from the temptation to say something.

It took several months of being amongst the burbling, warbling sprawl of other children to make him relax and try his hand at what everyone else was doing – talking to himself, calling out to others, chatting, speaking his pleasures and his irritations.

So, you certainly do not want to make the mistake of turning early language into a minefield where the child has to pick his way very carefully, thinking about every move before he makes it. You want it to be the means by which he can unselfconsciously communicate his feelings and interest in life.

Of course, a small child would understand what you meant by certain words even if you did not use baby-talk, because their understanding is more advanced than their ability to speak. The main reason for using baby talk is not that it teaches a child to *understand* but that it teaches him to *speak*. The repetition of simple words like "ta", "tum-tum", "gee-gee" and "ta-taa" gives him the chance to copy as they are within his range to imitate with comparative ease. Therefore they are stepping-stones in the process of learning to talk.

Also there is no need to look down on the invented words and abbreviations that families use. They help to breed their own atmosphere within a family which encourages children to be bold and free in making their own contributions to it. Baby words, in any case, tend to be gentle and caressing and that is the language of love at any age. They soften and personalise the language, making it more expressive to use.

Children who are not too "hag-ridden" about having to use the correct word for everything have more confidence in using language for their own ends and for improvising – sometimes unconsciously – to produce some lovely variations of their own.

We have collected some of our children's best ones over the years and they make beautiful examples of words being invested with even more meaning for a child despite being just off-centre. "Frightmares" for nightmares; "squirm" for worm; "pussy-pillar" for hairy caterpillars; "skellybones" for skeleton; "screwcrows" for scarecrows; "allibiters" for alligators; banana and "banapple"; and my son's unwittingly graceful compliment to food that looks lovely: "it's girlicious!"

You need have no fear that your child will continue with an infantile vocabulary into his teens! He will continue to say "bunny-rabbit" and "pussy-cat" for just as long as he enjoys the pretty sound of it and then he will drop the "bunny" and the "pussy". What he will retain, however, is a feeling for words that come trippingly off the tongue which will be constantly updated by his age and contact with other children.

There is another aspect of childish vocabulary which I would like to mention, if only because it has been the subject of so much academic and serious comment that many parents might feel afraid to follow their own inclination to ignore expert advice. That is the attitude you should take to words used for children's genitalia.

Ordinary families have always tended to use their own particular words to describe their "privy parts", knowing instinctively that biological words are only science working in its pedantic way without the sensitivity of true expression.

The fact that so many of these private words are humorous and oblique rather than scientific and "accurate" only reflects the fact that the organs and functions described are, indeed, very personal, and nothing can come between the individual and his own "naming of parts". Exactly the same scope for humour and individuality should be allowed for children who tend to go through a period of needing to talk quite a lot about such things.

It must be admitted that the only organ that really counts in this respect is the little boy's penis. Little girls just have a "bottom" and you get to know if they mean back or front! Funnily enough, doctors and nurses carry on this tradition as you notice when you have a baby; "How is your tail this morning?" being a common way professionals enquire about the state of stitches and general comfort; thus acknowledging the need to show a delicate unspecificness when dealing with individuals.

Little boys, however, seem to personalise their own organ and they often give it a name much as they do a favoured possession – and I can see nothing wrong in that. In my own family the four boys had four different words for it – none of them inherited from us – and the fact that one of them had a "tinkle" and one a "winkie" indicated to me that they like to keep their names subtly different.

It is no good pretending that, as a part of the body, it is no different from any other part. It is, and children know it. Any attempt to make it ordinary is as phoney as the sex educationalists who want us to pretend that sex is just a subject like any other. Since it is not, why pretend in the first place?

There is also one real disadvantage that I can see associated with children using biological or slang words for their genitals and bodily functions, and that is that when they use them in public, as is often the case, they can produce reactions of horror – rightly or wrongly – from those listening.

Once on a trip to the London Zoo we were watching the chimpanzees' tea party when an angelic little girl cried out with delight and excitement "Look at that monkey's big, red arse!", at which several people exclaimed in horror and did the equivalent of fainting away.

A child can be deeply impressed by such a reaction in others. The inexplicable disapproval can cause them considerable confusion and dismay. It is really not fair to leave your child open to such reactions, incurred in all innocence, just to satisfy your own desire for them to sound mature and enlightened.

The same problem arises with what word you should give your child to describe the function of defecating as well as the object itself! We have known several hilarious examples of progressive parents who, having spurned the homely "poo" as being too like baby-talk, were left with very few possible alternatives. "Mummy, I want to defecate" sounds too pretentious even for them; whilst "Tommy's done a stool in his pants" is just ridiculous.

So they have been left with only the word "shit" which is currently used as a coarse expletive, to express these natural and harmless functions. A case indeed where a euphemism is not only desirable but necessary!

Learning at home

The number of things a child has learnt by the time he goes to school is clearly phenomenal. Children's memories appear to be like a book that is open to the world. Everything they hear, see and experience is recorded on the pages without the slightest effort or difficulty.

Since a child is normally at home with his mother throughout this crucial time of learning and growth it is easy to see why the home is so essential as the very first learning environment.

However, there can be no hard and fast rules about what exactly constitutes the best and most stimulating circumstances for a child, except that it has very little to do with how much money you have.

It may be very pleasant to have a variety of toys and books with which to amuse a child (and they do as much to entertain the parent as anything) but they are no substitute for personal contact, conversation and genuine activity. It is not enough to have a brightly coloured, musical mobile hanging over the cradle if no face ever appears beside it to talk, smile and sing. Nor will it benefit the child much if he simply has toys to play with and no person.

The child learns in the first place from his mother – even as he lies in her arms being fed and talked to – and from those other people who take an active part in the life around him. From them he learns to love and respond, to listen and communicate, to look at colours and shapes, to separate individual objects from the mass around him, and slowly to imbibe the realities of the world.

In order to accomplish the seemingly enormous task of teaching a child all these things it is not necessary to be an incredible, textbook parent. In fact, it has got more to do with being natural and generous with your child by loving and having an interest in him than anything else; remembering to share with him your feelings and doings in order that he may first experience them and later reproduce them.

Fathers, in particular, often need to be reminded to show affection for their children and take an interest in them. Of course they are interested, but they may not show it because they somehow feel that the child cannot really understand them when they cannot speak and so they don't bother. They make elaborate plans instead about the coming days when they will show them how to play football or sail, or take them to parks and museums, and they rather miss the opportunity to establish an unselfconsciously close and affectionate relationship with their children.

"Teaching" young children is a question of making available the component parts that comprise everyday life – and that requires time far more than it does money. Look at pretty pictures together in books and magazines and stick them on the wall so you can point them out to each other during the day. Sing little things for the child's benefit as you go about your chores and get him to clap and bang things in accompaniment. Sing and dance with him in your arms – babies love that and it is good for their sense of rhythm.

Try and remember to count things out loud when you are laying them out and occasionally the stairs when you are going up and down. You will be amazed how quickly they realise what you are doing and grasp what numbers are.

Another thing that helps to organise their sense of number is to recite rhymes that itemise things. There are dozens of them, but my favourite came from my grandmother's grandmother and is rather solemn and fascinating to young children. You start with the thumb and move along the fingers:

> Thumbkin, thumbkin, broke the barn
> Pinnikin, pinnikin stole the corn
> Old Mid-man sat and saw
> Long-backed Grey carried it away
> And Peesey-weesey paid for all.

I cannot analyse the pleasure this rhyme gives children but it has little to do with understanding the meaning. It has a seriousness that certainly commended it to us more than jollier rhymes and, perhaps, also an unconscious sense that in childhood as well as in life, it is often Peesey-weesey who pays for all!

Another very great source of learning for a toddler is through helping with any jobs that are being done about the house. From the adult point of view, of course, it does not look as if he is doing very much – just pottering about with you or dad. But for the child it is a valuable way of learning a whole range of directed manipulative skills, muscle control and simply how to *do* things.

Give him a duster or a brush when you are cleaning so that he can follow around after you, and leave little piles of rubbish for him to put into the bin or sweep into the dustpan with a brush. Let him have a piece of pastry to play with when you are making it and give him the smallest cutter or egg-cup to press out the shapes with. Then he can decorate them with sultanas and sprinkle them with sugar to produce a fine effect. Even his grey, misshapen efforts will cook quite nicely alongside yours, and you can be sure that he will eat his own before he eats your superior ones.

Whatever you are doing in the kitchen give out some plastic bowls, a few implements and some spoons of different sizes to play with, and associate them with words like "big" and "small", "in" and "out", and colours. If they have not been too satiated with elaborate toys, children will exploit their potential to the full, They will spend time seeing which ones they can cram into each other, and whether they will stack. They will lay them out in lines, balance them and of course try the effect of banging and clattering them together.

It is perhaps difficult for someone who is not a parent to imagine what all this sort of activity can do for a child, but if you watch them carefully over a period you will notice their growing skill at handling things and the confidence that comes with identifying and separating out for themselves special things from the morass of objects around them.

A last word on vocabulary: it is well worth taking the trouble to tell even a toddler the proper names for some things. We tend, for example, rather unthinkingly, to lump all birds together, which is rather a wasted opportunity to expand word power since living things are always an area of high interest for a child and they love to be able to identify robins, thrushes, blue-tits, and blackbirds. Similarly the names of flowers are usually so beautiful in themselves that children love saying them. You do not have to be much of a gardening expert to know a rose when you see one, or daffodils, hollyhocks and forget-me-nots, and it gives them some lovely words to say.

Books, Stories and Television

It is often said that provided a child has knowledge of books he never falls behind other children in learning, even if he pays very little attention to any other lessons. If your child is going to be one of those who find reading for themselves very difficult and therefore boring, then reading a lot to him will help, not only to keep him abreast of children's literature, but also to give him a love of ideas and of different ways of expressing them.

You will probably start with simple books with pictures of things he likes and recognises such as animals, toys and everyday objects. Although they have no text, you can make up little comments and "plots" to match the mood of the moment and there is always something to talk about. You ask the child what he thinks the little dog is doing, sitting there. Is he waiting for his dinner, looking for his mummy, keeping his tail warm? It helps the child to be asked specific questions so that he can try and answer and express an idea or impart information.

Almost any picture has something in it that you can show a child and talk about, and there are so many beautiful postcards about that one is never at a loss. Paintings and scenes contain a lot of interesting material for a child and the colours and the people in them afford much pleasure. You can stick them on the kitchen wall at his eye level so that they will go on being a part of his consciousness.

By the time a child is three years old or thereabouts you will have gone through a good many of the colourful books with very little text that are the mainstay of the children's section in the library, and will be starting ones that can be read properly. Especially at first, you often find that children get to know their favourites by heart, and then you cannot change one word or syllable without their correcting you. I can still remember Beatrix Potter's *Miss Moppet* and *The Fierce Bad Rabbit* – even after several whiskeys and a few intervening years!

You can always read to a child at a higher level than he can speak himself because you can make the meaning clear by your tone of voice or by gestures and explanations. This holds true throughout childhood so it is very useful to continue it as a source of both pleasure and true education.

For some reason we have always gone for a sort of "core curriculum" of books in our family; reading and re-reading certain favourites out loud in an evening ritual that the children's enjoyment has rendered inescapable. It certainly deepens the experience of a book to read it many times and, if it is a classic of some kind, there is more to be discovered every time.

We particularly love the incomparable *Hucklebury Finn* and *Tom Sawyer, The Wind in the Willows,* all the Beatrix Potter and Alison Uttley books, all those by Edward Ardizzone, the "Narnia" books of C S Lewis, the "Just-So" stories, *The Jungle Book, Treasure Island,* and the eight books of Laura Ingalls Wilder about early pioneers in America. Later discoveries were *Stig of the Dump* and *The Otterbury Incident* by C Day Lewis, which joined the cycle of books which revolved once or twice a year. Children also love poetry if it is read to them, and Walter de la Mare's *Secret Laughter* is full of beautiful and haunting poems for children.

It must also be said, with more of a groan, that the younger children love "Noddy" and his gormless friend with the Big Ears! Having been unable to share their infatuation myself, despite several attempts, I have just had to learn to live with it. Like all Enid Blyton's books they are easy and enjoyable to read and, if not exactly imperishable classics, they seem to encourage children to read for themselves.

Once children have learnt to read and have settled into the habit, a whole new world is open to them. It is wonderful when they go off by themselves to read and the erstwhile noise of children playing together is replaced by the companionable silence of them all reading and looking at books.

It is very difficult to say exactly why reading is so different from watching television; but it is. Perhaps it is simply that there is nothing passive about reading, and you do not get up from a book feeling that you have merely been a spectator at events. You feel completely involved with the characters since you have given them all faces and movements and have dressed every scene yourself. You have expended some creative energy and because of it you have become a part of the book.

Also, of course, you do need to be interested in a book to make the effort to read it, whereas with television so much idle material can wash past you on the screen and you simply become too anaesthetised to switch it off.

For whatever reason, it is usually quite striking that children who read, or who are read to a good deal, reflect this by being more articulate, expressive and lively in their ideas than those children who simply watch a lot of television. It is not that you notice how clever they are – but how chatty and communicative they appear in comparison with most other children. I make this observation on my own behalf and must leave it to others to decide whether it is true in general and if their children are affected in this way.

I must also be honest and admit that I have a considerable dislike of television and its effects upon children. This is primarily because, as a medium, it demands such unhealthy passivity from its audience at a time when they should be doing things for themselves and creating their own imaginative world instead of being fed with whatever they happen to be given.

The second objection is just as important and I have an idea it will be found to be increasingly significant: that is the use made by television of violence, brutality and sex to make programmes more exciting.

It is the context of televisual violence that is so crucial: it is watched in the home, which is – in all other respects – the bastion of normality for a child. There on the screen, a place where he is used to seeing real things going on, a child regularly sees people smashing one another about, naked aggression or sadistic close-ups of injury. A child of two, three or four will look around to see what his parents are making of it all, and Mum will perhaps be sipping her tea and watching without obvious signs of shock and Dad is just leaning back smoking his pipe as usual. What is a child to deduce from it? He will not understand what is going on in the film, that is obvious, but what will he learn from the experience of watching injury and violence in an atmosphere of enjoyment at a time when his emotions and sensibilities are developing?

To an outsider who did not grow up with television, it seems so perverse and dangerous a habit to cultivate in children. If someone were to tell you that the first generation of young people who emerged into the world having been fed on this diet seemed to show a unique capacity to mindlessly smash and break things, to batter and bully the old, the young and the helpless, and to tolerate a far higher level of general violence than would have seemed believable to the generation immediately before them – you would not be surprised. Indeed, you would be inclined to say "Well, what do you expect?"

But cause and effect are notoriously difficult to prove in this as in other cases. In the end it comes down to common sense and common concern. One of the troubles is that so many people who should be more concerned with the business of protecting children from bad influences find it difficult to imagine the impact on young minds of such a diet of violence. To some extent, this is because they have been hardened by the same experience.

It is such a curious and unnatural pastime for young children to sit for hours at a time, watching aggression and violence for pleasure. Even the Romans, as far as I know, did not take their infants to watch gladiatorial conflicts and the Greeks in their plays were careful to keep all scenes of violence off-stage, only allowing the narrator to describe what was happening. Why were they so squeamish and we so hardboiled? Perhaps they discovered before us that violence breeds violence in more ways than one. Although watching violence may not be educating a child to be violent if that is not in his temperament or background, it is certainly getting him used to tolerating a high level of it.

The Greeks, with their overriding concern for citizenship, would have realised that society is a complex structure of checks and balances where one moderates one's behaviour to conform with the expectations of another. So complementary are these actions and reactions that one should *expect* that a society which has a high tolerance of violence will become one which has a high incidence of it also.

Of course the various TV networks have often countered the criticism that they show too much that is insensitive and brutalising by saying that they only transmit such programmes after nine o'clock. They thereby acknowledge that it is not a good thing to allow children to watch unsuitably violent or sexual material.

Their argument is that careful parents can avoid this dangerous contact by sending their children to bed. This is all very well and I've no doubt that most parents do, but it is not the children of careful parents that one has to be concerned about. By and large they are not going to be the ones who will destroy an orderly and peaceful society anyway.

The children one ought to be worrying about are precisely those children whose parents do not care what they watch any more than they know what they are up to at any time of the night or day. They are the delinquents of tomorrow and we are allowing them to be given a ready-made vocabulary of violence and sex and an appetite for aggression that no peaceful society can hope to satisfy.

It is, apart from anything else, a shockingly cynical attitude to plan programmes so that they protect well cared-for children, whilst leaving the already under-privileged exposed to acknowledged dangers. It is like discarding dangerous chemicals by putting them on a rubbish-dump where you know only the children of the poor will pick them over.

Perhaps the only poetic justice in the whole business is that the very liberals who oppose censorship even if it protects the vulnerable within the home, are probably the people who feel most acutely the creeping brutality of our times – even if they do not suffer from it the most. They can only agonise as more and more hitherto peaceful activities become dangerous or impossible – like watching football, rugby, cricket, fairs, carnivals or parades; and as churches, museums, gardens and beauty-spots have to be closed to the public unless they can be guarded. Even their most cherished crusades such as that for the equality of women, amount to nothing when the dangerous climate we have cultivated means that they are not even "equal" enough to go from A to B unaccompanied.

We got rid of our television when the eldest child was about eight years old and the main reason was the difficulty of stopping them from watching the children's programmes from the moment they came home from school until bed-time. There was literally no time for anything else like reading, talking or playing together.

Once the television had gone it was quite wonderful how our own atmosphere flowed back into the home. Only then did we realise how much the influence of television pervaded everything: that certain days mean certain programmes, and that one put off activities and cut short conversations according to the timing of this or that programme. Without it – oh bliss! One was so free.

Surprising as it may sound, the children did not miss it at all. They liked television and they still do, but when it was not there they simply got on with other things. It really has made a difference to them too. Obviously they read, talk and play more, and I know from friends that many children nowadays do not play extended or elaborate games, or tell stories or dress up to act out their favourite characters.

There are many things that children no longer do, or do very little, which were once considered to be very important for their growth and development, because television-watching has robbed them of the time and the inclination to do them. For some addictive reason, it is very difficult indeed to resist switching on the TV when you have one. One only has to be a little tired or bored and it becomes the easiest and most immediate option as well as being the ideal "child-minder". That is why we just took the plunge and got rid of it and then found that life was truly much better without it.

There are quite a lot of families like us who do not have TV and, talking to them, I have found their experience to be like ours – one of release. I only wish there were enough of us to persuade the BBC radio planners to do more to cultivate a listening public of the future by giving children at least some programmes.

It is quite scandalous that probably the best public broadcasting service in the world has got so few programmes for children per week. This is a ridiculous oversight in view of the fact that so many of the most popular children's classics would make equally enjoyable listening for adults.

One day, perhaps, someone at Broadcasting House will see this lack as a challenge and will turn their attention to it. When they do, they could well find that there is a much larger audience than they supposed for the kind of material that some of our best writers have provided for children, and that by cultivating a devoted young audience they would be helping to educate the next generation of regular radio listeners.

Imagination, religion and play

I wanted to put the subject of a child's imagination separately from that of simple learning because it is such a powerful faculty that it deserves consideration on its own.

To say that children have strong imaginations is really to underestimate the scope of the word. It would be truer to say that their minds are only partially what we would call rational at all, with another side that is dominated by the imagination. In a child this is the means by which he keeps his perceptions receptive as to what the world conveys to him and what he is going to find meaningful in life. The world is full of possibilities to a child, more full than an adult can ever remember, and many options are kept open as to what is true and false by the imaginative framework in which they are set.

Thus, for example, I would still maintain that I believe in fairies because the difference between whatever they are and what poets describe in other terms as "unseen forces" and "the spirit of nature" are so slight. We feel those forces as adults, and as children we personify them as fairies, elves, gnomes and pixies. They fit exactly the different moods that one finds in nature and feels in a landscape, and they reflect more or less accurately man's preoccupation with the living world of nature.

We were talking once at home about the way some children at school discounted all the tales and legends about super-nature when William said, in a burst of insight into his own feelings, "I believe in everything!"

To deny the existence of witches, mermaids, trolls and wood-nymphs as well as the aforementioned fairy-folk would be to dismiss an area of thought that is vivid with sensations and experiences.

Children do not need to have it explained to them that the reason woods, water, field and forest have super-natural beings associated with them is because they have a beauty that is powerful and deep and needs to be personified before people can handle it.

Recognising and identifying with the "bubbles under the surface" of material things is a significant part of a child's imagination. Another part deals with the dark fears and imaginings that most children seem to have. Unlikely as it seems, they are quite preoccupied at times with the subjects of death, destruction, maiming and grief, and these have to be brought out in the open in order to be dealt with.

Most cultures have the means of personifying and structuring these fears in the form of stories and folk tales which deal with them. It is a fairly harrowing experience for an adult to read a book of Grimm's fairy tales to children: personally I find the cloying, morbid atmosphere most depressing. But children do not complain at the gloom and the "cri-cri-croo, there's blood in the shoe!" nor the heavy, inexorable pace of retribution. To them it is like someone rearranging heavy furniture; they are using large symbols to represent things that loom large in their minds.

Their interest in death does seem inexplicable to adults who must be too far away from childhood to remember what it was like. I have often wondered whether it is to do with the fact that they have only quite recently "come alive" themselves and they still feel the lack of memory of the past and the shadow of the womb.

Also children must see death as a very arbitrary and random visitation. Even a dead wasp lying on the path can raise the question, "Where has it gone?"

"Nowhere, it's just dead, that's all."

"By why is it dead?"

"Well" (thinks) "things die all the time. Perhaps he was old, or sick or" (lamely) "perhaps he had an accident."

"But where do your *insides* go when you're dead?"

"They don't go anywhere. It's like a machine that stops. That's all."

Whew! It is amazing how difficult some of their simple questions can be to answer. One certainly realises how little we question or understand things around us. Only certain occasions, or children wanting answers, makes us cast around for explanations.

However simple and truthful one tries to be in answering such questions from a child, the sheer arbitrariness of it all creates anxiety in their minds which makes them want to talk about it. Perhaps also there is the half-felt thought that "if it could happen to a wasp it could happen to me".

Therefore, having no framework of their own to attach it to, children explore the subject through stories. These folk tales have a beginning and an end instead of being a worrying continuum and, which is also a help, they happen to someone else so it is an experience shared by others.

Another potent function of the imagination in children is its use to animate objects. This starts at more or less the same time as a child begins to communicate with people and is perhaps simply a practising process tried on something which cannot get away.

Or perhaps it is that children only relate to inanimate or non-human things by seeing them first as people. They will, for some time, blame a "stupid chair" for bumping them and will even smack and kick some object which has been the means of giving them pain.

The way in which a baby of a few months old plays with a rattle shows he has infused it with life. They are playing together so he talks to it and it waggles in response. He is able to animate anything and everything so that they are not mere boring objects but are things with which he can have a relationship.

You can put a puppet on your hand for a two-year-old and, though he is well aware of your hand going into it and the fact that you are doing the talking, he will become completely involved with the toy in a way that shows it is quite real to him. It is not, as it is with adults, "willing suspension of disbelief" for he has no disbelief to suspend. The world of the imagination is the one in which he lives.

It must be this power that we have as children that lingers in our personification of "old father time" and "mother nature" as well as the innumerable stories, both adult and childish, that are about animals and objects that talk. We are unconsciously drawing upon our recollections of a time when the world really did appear like that for us. For children there is nothing unusual in having animals, broomsticks, trees, flowers and motor cars that talk; they are all part of their world.

In particular, the relationship children have with animals as talking creatures is a rich and important one. Because the animals feel and, to some extent behave like human beings, a child is able to enter their world and to sympathise with them. Peter Rabbit must do more to give a child a true picture of the warmth and vulnerability of animals, their worth and separate existence, than any diagram or plain photograph ever could.

All good stories that use animals in this way are imparting the truth to children by means of the imagination. Everything that feeds that sympathetic imagination is vitally important since it serves to deepen what is essentially a spiritual perception of things. We *feel* with them instead of just knowing about them.

There are many beautiful books of animal stories in the English language and I'm sure our national battiness about animals has been educated and reinforced by these innumerable classics. They serve a serious purpose for older children because they involve them in the lives of the animals so that their sympathy for these and for all living creatures can be extended. By describing accurately and dramatically the details of animal life they teach respect and love of them. It is by the power of the imagination that animals are given their place of importance in our world.

For whatever age group they are primarily intended, the best of such children's books are important stepping stones into feelings and understanding. When one comes again to read Beatrix Potter, Kenneth Grahame or A A Milne, after a gap of perhaps twenty years since you first heard them from your mother or teacher, one is struck by how serious they are at times. It is as if the author, in re-tracing the steps he took as a child, finds himself faced by the same bridge that he had to cross once before and which took him, inexorably, into another, less amiable world.

It is an indication of their integrity as writers that such authors do not duck the occasion but tell the children that, like dear little Pigling Bland, "once you have crossed the county boundary you can never go back again".

Once children have crossed over the bridge from childhood into the adult world, animals still have a part to play in educating their feelings. Both Kipling and C S Lewis use them, as old companions, to plot a course through the more difficult problems that arrive with adult life, and it seems natural for them to do so.

Religion

As for the place of religious teaching in a child's life – I simply cannot imagine trying to rear a child without it. Children are so primeval themselves, preoccupied with death and destruction and fascinated by blood. It is obviously a necessity for them to talk about and come to terms with the basic facts of life and death because these things matter to them.

Christianity talks as much about death and suffering, lepers, cripples, the sick, the blind, the bad and the mad as any child could need and it puts them all in a context of love and concern. It also provides, through the Resurrection, the relief of a hopeful end to suffering which becomes part of a child's way of looking at life.

Whether one is religious oneself, or whether one sees religion as a social myth that helps one to cope with life's extremes – it seems to me that children need it to help them grow up and they have a right to be acquainted with it as part of their education.

It is useless to pretend that rearing a child as an agnostic, or a believer in nothing at all, involves telling a child *less* that is fanciful or untrue. The questions children ask are very basic; such as why did a friend's baby have such a long illness and die? Or where is Grandma now? And agnostics are no more certain of the answers than anyone else. They too can only express an opinion and it is one which offers little comfort to a child.

I honestly do not know what you would say to a child who was bereft at the death of a pet unless you could say that they too would be a part of any heaven occupied by human beings. How much more difficult to present them with the death of a relative or a friend without that same promise of everyone being together again one day. Children accept this comfort as readily and naturally as adults, and I cannot imagine why anyone should want consciously to deprive them of it. There are many fears and lonelinesses in childhood that adults never get to hear of, and a loving Father in Heaven and a gentle Mother have been the refuge and strength of many a miserable and uncertain child.

Many undecided or agnostic parents do understand this need for independent comfort for their children and would like to provide them with it, but do not have the knowledge or experience of religion to pass on to them.

That is probably why, in quite a few homes, death is an absolutely taboo subject – particularly when it has occurred in the family. My children know, at this moment, more than one family where the recent death of a relative is not spoken of in the house when the adults and children are together, but is discussed in whispers by the children behind a tree at the end of the garden rather as the subject of "where babies come from" was by an earlier generation.

A culture like ours which has temporarily lost its religious imprint finds it difficult to offer guidelines on the subject of death because there is no easy answer that materialism can give. Just how easy it is to make mistakes because of this cultural vacuum was brought home to me when our cat was knocked down on the road and killed.

It was a Saturday morning and all the children were enjoying a slight lie-in when my neighbour dashed in to tell me that she had seen our poor cat, Sheba, lying on the kerb and obviously dead. She had four kittens only a few weeks old, and we knew how upset the children would be, so I gladly accepted her offer to collect the body and dispose of it in her dustbin.

I told the children when they came down to breakfast and there was much sadness and tears, and then they went upstairs to feed the kittens with milk and a dropper. After an hour or so had passed they came downstairs again and asked me where Sheba was. I told them what our neighbour had done and that I had been worried about them being upset seeing Sheba all bloodied and knocked about. "Well, of course we will be upset", they said, "but she is *our* cat".

I suddenly saw very clearly what they were trying to express. That because she was our cat and we loved her, we had to grieve over her too when she died. It was a part of the responsibility of owning her in the first place and part of the relationship with her. To deny the expression of it just because it was painful was to suppress feelings that very much needed to be expressed.

So we went and collected her, and the children unwrapped her from the newspapers and laid her out in a box. It was sad and painful, but everyone felt so much better after she had been consigned to a grave under a tree in the garden. "Now we've done the job properly", as my son put it, and they all got on with seeing that the kittens survived.

Since this is a book about bringing up children, here is no place to argue the relative merits of a religious education, except in that context. So it is appropriate to remark only that I believe that a child's moral sense is fed by the mutually understood, long-term traditions and stories that are contained within the Bible. But even more than this, the Christian religion teaches children an idealism and hope about life that they cannot easily discover any other way. Practical experience will show them that not all people are good and, as they grow older, the amount of evil in the world may well cause them to have a morbid and even despairing view of human life.

They need to be *taught* an alternative optimism that gives them a clear idea of what goodness is and how it works. To put it simply, they need to see clearly that there are two paths and that, however bad the world may appear, and however awful people may be to them at times, there is another way that *they* can take into something kinder and more hopeful. This encourages a vigorous, fighting attitude to life rather than the cynicism and impotence that so many young people fall into today; a feeling that they have no personal destiny to fulfil.

A religious education is also a vivid way of imparting shared values that a child will see referred to and reinforced by the Christian traditions that abound everywhere. Of course, in a Buddhist or Hindu culture those religions would be evidenced and shared, but I can see no point in putting all religions on the same footing in one's own culture since that is likely to make them all seem equally artificial and irrelevant rather than uniquely worthwhile. Apart from anything else, a child who loves and appreciates his own religion is likely to be respectful of the religious beliefs of others, which is very important in a society where many religions are represented.

In the end, of course, all children will come to make up their own minds about their need for religion and nothing you can say or do will alter that. But religion has in common with other subjects the fact that you need to know something about it; to be familiar with it in order to assess its worth and importance.

The Bible teaches brotherly love and lively moral sense in a moving and memorable way so that, at the very least, even if the faith that animates it should fall away in adult life, what is left will be a conscience that has been stimulated and informed by many profound examples.

In any case, it is noticeable that when children are brought up without any religion at all they are not, in consequence, any less superstitious or credulous than their fellows. Since children actually *are* superstitious and credulous, it is far better for them to have something worthwhile to believe in rather than filling the vacuum with third-rate mysticism dreamed up by the makers of films and comics just to fulfil their longing for transcendental experience.

The alternative is the situation revealed by a teenage magazine which polled its readers on the subject. Though a majority of them dismissed the idea of there being a God, they believed in the Devil, ghosts and even monsters! It is a classic example of G K Chesterton's famous observation that when people no longer believe in God, they will not believe in *nothing* – they will believe in *anything!*

Play

The last topic I want to mention on the subject of imaginative learning is the phenomenon of play. We tend to think of play as being much like resting or being asleep; that is, as an alternative to activity and as lightweight and inconsequential. However, it is not all it seems, and if you observe closely what is going on during certain games, you will see that, psychologically, it is as important to children as nutrition and exercise are to them physically.

I only really started to notice the content of children's games by accident because our bedroom window overlooked that part of the garden where they usually played. The window is covered by a net curtain and so I spent many hours sitting unobtrusively feeding a baby and watching the play developing.

Some games are straightforward affairs of fun and letting off steam and energy. In these you notice more than anything how the little ones gravitate towards the older ones who do things better than they do, and how, even in this, they unconsciously create a learning situation.

The most skilful at any particular activity becomes the centre of attention and the skill is copied down the line to a greater or lesser degree. Even competitiveness, seen in its early stages in young children, is all about learning. They compete in order to improve themselves. Without someone to compete with, they have no standard to apply to themselves to see how they are doing.

Even more interesting than these extrovert, physical games, however, are the serious ones played with much dedication from about the age of three until eleven or twelve.

In these games, each of the children is given a part in a quick and uncontentious way by the child who is initiating the game. There is some discussion about the direction the story should take and the one who initiates it is always deemed to know more about it than anyone else.

"You be the doctor and I'm the mummy coming to see you with my little boy; and he doesn't want an injection; and you say he's got to have one; and his dog rescues us because you're really a witch."

Then off they will go with this piece of drama being altered and modified by the characters as they go along; little boy does not want a dog, he wants a lion.

"Don't be silly, you can't have a lion."

"Yes I can, because we live in a zoo and my dad lets me play with the lions." (Perfectly reasonable, OK let's carry on!)

This kind of play has a very substantial purpose for children which is why they take it so seriously and never seem to take it into their heads to laugh at one another's ideas or acting abilities. It is rather like a game of chess to them because they are exploring possibilities and devising strategies for coping with the world.

Very often the scenes they enact contain several adults and they try out ways of dealing with them and relating to them. They invariably use the adults they know as models and it is very disconcerting to hear one's own querulous, corrective platitudes reproduced so perfectly by one's children in the course of a game.

This activity is obviously so important to children because, in such scenes, they are able to control events and so prevent themselves from being overwhelmed. *They* control what happens in the course of a game very subtly and precisely by the running commentary that sustains the action. The moment the going gets too hard and the bad man they have set up gets too nasty, for example, they will all connive at destroying him, either by intelligent means or, if that fails, by foul; even disposing of him if necessary with a magic stick.

Another interesting thing I used to notice during these watching-while-feeding sessions was that the overriding factor in deciding who would play what role was not gender, but energy and spirit. "She can't be Little John, she's too much of a cry-baby" could just as easily be: "He can't be Robin Hood, he can't run fast enough."

However, for some reason, boys will not play girls' parts except for laughs, whereas girls are perfectly happy to play the part of men. I don't think this can be explained in terms of "social conditioning" and the supposed low status of women because, to boys and girls of this age, their mothers are probably the most admirable, powerful and influential figures in their lives.

Perhaps this is the answer: that so great is the aura of femaleness that surrounds a mother to her children that boys do not even attempt to identify with it, whilst girls do not have the same inhibitions about reproducing what they identify as male characteristics.

Whatever the reason, the same pattern persists when they are older and boys cannot see themselves as women – even courageous or heroic ones like Grace Darling or Boadicea – but girls are quite happy to dress and seem as men.

I have never been very convinced by the arguments for the so-called social conditioning of children. Personally I have never been able to "socially condition" my boys to remember to wash their faces before going out, despite daily propaganda. Besides, in most other things, people tend to agree that trying to condition youngsters away from their innate desires only produces the opposite result; so why should it be any different in sex stereotyping?

Some things, whether we like it or not, are just so basic to a particular child, or to children in general, that there is nothing we can do to alter them. One can only alter *oneself* to accept them, which is a much easier task in comparison.

Pre-school education

One cannot talk about children without discussing, however briefly, the education they will receive from agencies outside the home. I am not planning to discuss the subject of primary and secondary schooling because it is somewhat outside the scope of this book, which is based primarily on the home-centred business of child rearing.

However, the pre-school playgroup age is an excellent "cutting-off" point for this enterprise since children are still predominantly in the home environment but with the outlines of the proper school experience forming in their minds.

As an institution, playgroups are firmly established now, and one of the best things about them is how much they vary. They are, for the most part, privately run by women who have, or who have had, children of their own. They reflect not only the personal philosophy of the people who run the group but also the feelings and attitudes of the small communities they serve.

They are much more accessible to parents than schools usually are: a major reason for this is that mothers do not feel over-awed by the mystique of professionalism that schools so assiduously foster. If you would really like your child to be doing something more constructive in the mornings or you are not happy about the standard of behaviour that seems to be allowed, you can discuss it woman to woman with the person in charge without undue fuss.

Whether the school is small or spacious, disciplined or free, learning- or play-oriented, the child, if he is ready, will derive a good deal of pleasure from it. Children have two important things to experience at this time as a prelude to "big" school, and one is being part of a group rather than being on a one-to-one basis with mother all the time.

The second is doing things with children of the same age and learning from equals and not from elders and betters. Even if the child comes from a large family his siblings will be older – with the possible exception of a baby – but he will be used either to having allowances made for him all the time or never being able to do as well as the others. Either way, slight adjustments have to be made and this is probably easier in a small, informal group rather than in the larger, altogether more alarming reception class of a school.

I have always thought it is a great shame that playgroups in general have not utilised more systematically a young child's tremendous learning abilities.

Their capacities at this age are immense and they learn words, phrases, songs, stories and rhymes by heart and at the drop of a hat. They can learn numbers with equal ease if they are taught them.

When my children were all at pre-school age, a friend and I ran a playgroup in our village hall. We always had a sitting-down session about halfway through the morning and we were amazed at how good the children's memories were when the material was systematically presented.

It did not matter how many rhymes we said, they knew them all by heart after two or three repetitions, with the quickest leading the slower ones. We added two or three new ones every week and still never got to the end of their ability to absorb everything we gave them. It seemed to be both effortless and natural to them, particularly if there were accompanying movements that fixed the images in their minds.

Soon we took to using a big abacus at these sessions and found that counting together is a wonderful exercise. Firstly, it is a terrific way of practising clear speech for any child who has difficulty in that direction – and many do at this age. If they are often corrected at home for saying a word wrongly, they may be unwilling to demonstrate the weakness in front of the other children. Speaking in a group therefore lessens their self-consciousness and enables them to practise difficult sounds.

You can further distract their attention away from their problem by varying the way you count. Since there are no particular images attached to numbers you can count in a variety of ways that do not detract from the sense of what you are saying. Loudly, softly, crossly, happily, sloppily or very clearly – you can practice in any tone you like, ringing the changes and adding to vocabulary, expression, fluency and confidence whilst committing the numbers firmly to memory.

There are a remarkable number of interesting things to count when just sitting down together: faces, ears, ribbons, fingers, brown shoes, blue eyes, doors, lights and windows. You can make the children look around them carefully by these means, to notice and isolate the component parts of their environment.

You can start to play "I Spy", and the beginnings of learning the alphabet. *I spy with my little eye something beginning with 'D'* (the sound, not the letter). The children understand within minutes that it is "door" you are after, and they get very good at it. Just a few little rounds of the game every day and it is amazing how much basic learning can be painlessly accomplished without their even being aware of it.

Our biggest problem at our little playschool was the children whom we called "telly-puddled". We often did not know the full story of what made them so dull, but they certainly never seemed to do anything but watch TV.

The consequence of this was that they did not know what books were for, but fingered them gingerly and in a desultory fashion because they were quite unaware that they were potentially interesting.

Even more disturbingly, they did not know how to play. Quite literally! They would show no desire to put their hands in the sand tray or to ride a bicycle around, but would sit, quite happily but entirely passive as if waiting for something to happen. They had to be shown at some length what to do with bricks and sand, cars and paint and then they would slowly awaken and begin first to actively watch and then to copy the others.

It was even more difficult, of course, to get these children interested in books as they really could not see the point of them at all! We had to start with them firmly clamped to the knee whilst we read in ecstatic and, at times hysterical, tones from something highly-coloured and action-packed. They would gaze into our faces with mild surprise for a time before slowly making the connection between our frenzied monologues and what was going on in the book. Thereafter, one built slowly on this interest and I never found a child who could not be hooked on the medium given time.

It was very significant that unless we insisted, these children would not have put themselves out to learn. If left to their own devices, the children from homes where they are shown the pleasures of the mind and who thereby have such a head-start, would have stayed with us to learn while the children who desperately needed the help would have been content endlessly to ride a bicycle around.

Another problem commonly experienced by all people teaching pre-school tinies is the child who does not want what you have to offer! This child seems oblivious to all the trouble you have gone to preparing the sand trays and water, and little pots of paint leave him quite indifferent. He does not appreciate at all what he will gain from a morning's activities with other children because all he wants at that moment is his mother and his home and he yells the place down to get them.

There generally seem to be two kinds of child who do this, and one is the sort who does not like his routine changed. He is like an old man wanting things the same as they have always been. He may scream and cry and generally make an awful fuss but one is aware that, underneath all the noise, a strong, integrated spirit is coping all right and he will be interested in other things after the shock of change is over. The actual moment of parting from mum or dad is often the signal for tears to start even though, as the worried parent will often tell you, they were quite happy on the way there. It is just as well to recognise this feeling that "parting is such sweet sorrow" and avoid protracted farewells which make leave-taking so painful. It is, after all, not only children who dislike saying goodbye. Most of us have experienced at some time the ineffable sadness of seeing a loved one go out of sight, even when we are going to see them later that day!

Once the parent is out of sight, recovery can be very rapid. So rapid in fact that we asked worried mothers on many occasions to go round to a side window two minutes after leaving a tearful child at the front door, to witness how the child became cheerful and occupied the moment the traumatic parting was over.

The other kind of child who cries is the one who is just too young for the experience of playgroup. Most children seem "to ripen" for a parting from their mother at around three years old, give or take a few months. They are just ready for it then, rather in the way that they suddenly mature into a state of balance and can then walk at a little over a year old. It makes no difference, in the case of walking, whether they are slightly built or have legs like tree trunks or whether you try to teach them to walk. When they are ready an inner realignment takes place and they are off with no looking back.

There is nothing you can do for the child who is too young to be in a playgroup. When the parent goes he is bereft and nothing you can do will console him. Once protest has been exhausted for the morning – and that can last a very long time – it is replaced by a sort of fragile apathy that is not good to see. You know that the child is getting nothing from the experience but, on the contrary, is laying down memories and sensations that will probably disturb his peace of mind in years to come.

It is far better, in these circumstances, to take the child back home and forget about playgroup for a while. It does not matter if he never goes to one providing he has a normally interesting and stimulating home life. It is something in which it is better to be guided by your own feelings and instincts rather than by rigid guidelines. It does not follow that, because your child does not like playgroup, he will continue the struggle to stay at home when the time comes to start school. The passing of even a few months makes an enormous difference at this age and with children then being very definitely old enough to survive, you can reassure them with a confidence that carries conviction. They usually love primary school once they have had the time to settle into the routines and to accept the inescapable regularity of going five days a week. As our son, Riffen – who was convinced he had a medical condition which rendered him allergic to school – was once heard to tell a friend; "It must have been ever so much worse being a galley slave in ancient Rome".

'Sex education'

The imparting of knowledge about sex to children is the last aspect of "education" that I would like to discuss since it always seems to appear under this heading even though, in its wider context, it does not properly belong there.

Most of the advice offered to parents by experts in the field is along the lines that children should be told "everything", which is bound to make most parents feel that they are not competent to do the job! What is "everything" after all? The very idea makes the mind boggle.

Even those parents who were brought up in the "swinging sixties" when everyone learnt how to be uninhibited and frank about all sorts of things, seem to suffer from the same shortcomings that their poor repressed parents were accused of by an earlier generation of sex educationalists.

The conclusion I came to long ago was that it was the "sexperts" themselves who were abnormal and out of step with everybody else because of their obsessive desire to isolate and concentrate upon sex. The fact that so few of them seem to have normal feelings of reticence or modesty which are common to almost everybody else and to all cultures, should be regarded as a symptom of mania rather than a healthy attitude. It should never be allowed to make parents feel abnormally prudish in their attitudes and so unfit to talk to their children about personal matters.

Time and again in the course of teaching English to children over sixteen years old, we came across either explicitly or obliquely sexual scenes in books which required some kind of comment, and I was struck by how sensitive the majority of students are towards such personal matters being too obviously exploited. Children are just as likely to feel diffident and shy about some aspects of sex as their parents are, which is all the more reason not to leave them to the tender mercies of the sexual hearties to whom nothing is either delicate or sensitive.

Do we have such a thing as a "sex-life" that is distinct from our other life? Is there such a thing as "sexual activity" that is not connected also to our reason and our emotions? What can you possibly teach truthfully about sex that is not also a lesson about the infinite variety of men and women? Even the fact that in a sex lesson some children will be enjoying it whilst to others it is a painful experience should tell a sensitive teacher that this is not a "subject" at all and that any attempt to treat it as such is a lie and a pose.

There are, of course, certain biological facts to do with human growth, development and reproduction which can be taught as part of the biology lesson without causing anyone dismay, and this is the way it was done, unremarked, for years. Some shaky diagrams on the board and in our books and a few labels added in more or less the right place and it was all over. One could even forget about it for a few years if one wanted to!

The "facts of life" were got across in school at some point in a continuing story of learning about human relationships in the company of the people who understand and describe them best: storytellers, poets, artists and the writers of songs and ballads.

For the rest, the kinds of questions that children ask can only be properly answered by their parents because only they can guess what lies behind the question and what sort of answer the child needs.

Even they can make mistakes sometimes – a friend told me once, how her son had returned from school and had asked his father where he came from.

"This is it!" thought dad. "The moment has come for me to tell him "the facts of life" really beautifully". So he took his son for a walk around the allotments and when they came back with the job well done, he asked his son what had made him ask the question at that particular moment.

"Oh well", his son replied, "my friend John Scott says he comes from Yorkshire and I wondered where we came from. That's all!"

Certainly children ask questions about where babies come from and these should be answered as simply and straightforwardly as possible. However, you must use your knowledge of the child to determine how comprehensive your explanation should be.

In asking that question, for instance, many children will only want you to confirm that the baby is carried in your tummy and would not dream of asking how he got out. They prefer perhaps to imagine for themselves the most comfortable way out that does not make them feel anxious.

I looked after two little boys for a day once when their mother was taken to hospital to have a baby. She had carefully prepared them for the event by watching with them television programmes about childbirth which featured several babies being born.

These little boys were aged about five and seven years old and, to my astonishment, as soon as they arrived they started to tell me how a doctor with a big, black bag was going to come to their mummy and give her a little baby out of it.

I was completely mystified by these explanations although I tried not to show it, and wondered if they could have possibly forgotten all they had seen. The very urgency of their manner, however, was like someone desperately trying to forestall any other explanation and I suddenly realised that they could not bear to imagine their mother involved in the worrying process they had seen on the screen. They had simply "edited out" the knowledge for their own peace of mind and were vastly relieved and contented when I did not attempt to correct them but accepted their story without surprise.

Allowing children's imaginations room to manoeuvre is very important. There will always be some children who need to soften, or even alter the facts if they are worried by them and you should recognise and accommodate this sensitivity if it is there.

I would go further than that. I have a very definite instinct which tells me that not allowing children to opt out from sexual knowledge if they want is dangerous for their state of mind.

They have the ability *not* to register what they do not want to know even when it is taking place all around them, and this is a defence mechanism which should be allowed to function naturally and without interference from adults.

If you have not told them enough about something or other, children will continue with the questions until they get the full picture they are after. They are much more unhappy and disturbed – which, of course, they cannot explain to adults – if they are not actually ready for all that you have unloaded onto them.

For this reason, I do not think it is a good idea to tell young children about the role of the father in conception. They do not have the emotional framework in which to put this information and I cannot see how it can do anything but worry them because they cannot really understand it. It is always received at quite another level from the adult one and no one can be sure what goes on in the individual child's mind.

Certainly when they ask – in relation to babies in tummies – "How does it get there?" what they have in mind is some simple cause and effect explanation, like "God put him there" or if you prefer it "Nature put him there".

It strikes me as very unfeeling, not to say unkind, to answer such an obvious query with all the unlikely facts about human copulation and conception. That really is more than they could have bargained for.

What is more, to put a child in possession of such remote, peculiar and even unlikely facts is to risk making him wary of the whole topic. What is preferable is for their confidence and interest to keep pace with their ability to understand what they learn.

That innocent confidence is so well displayed by the anecdote concerning the children of the Victorian, Lord Lytton. They organised a charade which showed a Crusader returning after many years from the wars full of tales about his exploits and achievements. His fond wife duly responded to this by opening the door of the nursery and showing him several lovely children with the words, "As you can see, Sir, I too have not been idle".

This confident innocence both pleases and amuses adults primarily because it is a healthy sign of a child who is not confused or intimidated by what he knows. We respond instinctively to this state of well-being and feel that it is a natural strength.

I believe strongly that children should be allowed to remain secure in their innocence for as long as childhood genuinely lasts. The advantages far outweigh the disadvantages particularly, in the first instance, for little girls.

Childhood is a time of genuine sexlessness. That is not to say that there are no sexual differences or that children do not have sexual feelings; they obviously do, but they are undirected and easy to sublimate and distract into other channels while the child does not know their significance.

They are sexless in the sense that, in many ways, they are neither very strongly male or female and so are without inhibiting "role" attitudes. They romp and rough-house together much as they do in playschool and are quite unaware of any implications of their actions.

That is all over once the heavy body of sex information descends upon them. The headmaster of a primary school told me approvingly that the only effect he had detected in his eight-year-old pupils after their sex education programme was that they refused to get changed for games together in the classroom as they used to do, but separated into the toilets to do it. What an ass the man must have been to take pleasure in seeing the freedom of innocence replaced by fear and shame.

It is particularly unfortunate for little girls to be given the sobering burden of the facts about menstruation, puberty and childbearing when they are still at the carefree stage at which they think of themselves as being much like boys.

The suffocating pall of what our culture calls "femininity" closes round them soon enough. The separateness of their role is then emphasised by every vested interest trying to sell them the means to achieve it to the required standard. They are remorselessly groomed by these mainly commercial pressures into thinking of themselves as existing primarily for the purpose of attracting the opposite sex by their shape, appearance and smell. It is not surprising if boys come, in time, to think of them in the same way.

The years before puberty are a time in which children are free to develop themselves along lines that are not prescribed by their biological functions. The longer that freedom is allowed to continue, the more chance there is of a more free spirit developing to a state where it can better withstand the pressure to conform.

It is true, of course, that most girls have an absorption in their appearance from an early age which derives from an instinctive knowledge that their looks are a gift, along the lines of the biblical "talents", which they will use for good or ill.

It is not possible to dismiss this absorbed self-interest as merely socially conditioned. One of the children that I "baby-minded" some years ago was the 18-month-old daughter of an intellectual feminist who would not be seen dead in either a brassière or a skirt. Her little girl, on the other hand, loved to sit in front of a mirror sticking little pieces of cotton wool into her hair and turning her head coquettishly from side to side watching the effect.

Her parents were rather aghast, I think, until they came to accept that to imagine you can produce at will children who are carbon copies of your own beliefs and attitudes is to be contemptuous of their individuality as well as unrealistic. Now they have a little boy as well whose bombast and almost stereotyped masculinity makes his mother blanch at times.

The little girl refuses to wear trousers on the grounds that they are ugly and can only be induced to wear a pair that are very frilly or very pink – or both.

In fact, the point that the parents in this case ought to be deriving satisfaction from is that both children are sufficiently independent-minded to be themselves. In the long run it is their sense of independence that makes children develop in accordance with their own temperament and preferences and not in response to pressure either from a stereotyped culture or from radical parents whose pressure can be even worse.

However, having said that little girls have an innate interest in their appearance, it does not follow that this should become the dominant or exclusive concern of their lives. Even if you do not allow any of the sillier girls' magazines into your house, they will still encounter them at school or with friends; and the preoccupation with personal vanity that, for purely commercial reasons, they exploit, should be fought with frequent recourse to sound reason and humorous scorn.

It is such a waste when their real desire to be interesting and valuable to people is distorted into an obsession with their personal appearance that leaves many other areas underdeveloped.

That boys are different from girls in many respects, basically and, intrinsically, need not be argued with anyone who has direct experience of children – or indeed eyes in their head! It does not therefore come as much of a surprise that, as adults, they turn out to be different from one another in ambitions, interests and pursuits.

It is difficult to see how the concern to identify so-called "sexist bias" in books and learning materials for children is going to alter the basic fact that most of the items found are an accurate reflection of a preference that already exists in children.

I have never understood why it is that little boys love machinery and anything that whirrs, bangs or speeds about. My own sons are just the same and yet their father is allergic to machinery and is never seen with anything more masculine than a paintbrush in his hands. In the end, one is bound to concede that their basic interests will predominate in what they do and even the non-stop "conditioning" of home life is not sufficient to alter or disguise that permanently.

Once again, therefore, the key to a child's self-fulfilment is likely to be that he has the confidence and the strategy to go the way he really wants, regardless of other people's beaten tracks.

A girl who really wants to become an engineer can do so if she applies herself – just as boys have been able to become successful cooks and dress designers without having had the benefit of their teachers and their families expecting it from an early age.

Many children of both sexes have a far harder struggle against family expectations based on class and background than they ever do from sex stereotyping. A working-class child who wants to go into painting or poetry has about as much difficulty as a child from a county background who wants to become a social worker.

An area of concern for present-day parents is the horrible tendency in our culture – particularly in that part of it which is directed towards the young – to foster fantasy as opposed to reality.

This is prejudicial to children's development because, after a prolonged diet of the same thing, they become separated from *themselves* and cannot therefore mature towards sensible goals. As you might expect, this fantasy intake is in different forms for boys and girls, with boys going for a diet of conflict and violence in their magazines and girls to endless rehearsals of being discovered and then loved by someone. Both sexes come together on the silver screen where a combination of all these elements preoccupies them more than anything else.

It is a vast subject and not one that I intend to cover thoroughly because, quite honestly, it is beyond my range. However, any parent is in a position to judge the debilitating effect upon a child when daydreaming becomes too much of a habit. It is always a sign of something wrong and sometimes this may just be that the child is under-occupied or not happy at what he is doing.

Good books have the effect of stimulating the mind and the imagination whereas vacuous magazines provide only an escape from the effort of doing anything in your life. In this way, a child's head can be so full of vivid fantasies for weeks and months that he cannot contemplate doing anything so boring as cleaning out his guinea-pigs' cage. Real life can never compete with a fantasy world, and if they get too much of it, children and young people can actually find themselves alienated from their own lives and from reality.

I have actually noticed young girls whose heads are so stuffed with fantasies about their appearance, its effect and conquests that they cannot be made to think of anything else, even when they are intelligent and their futures depend upon it.

A similar observation, made in the days when I used to help run a youth club, is that boys who become addicted to a diet of violence in their young days, progress to soft and hard pornography as the next step upwards in their fantasy life.

They cannot enjoy contact with reality and have a need to turn people and events into a series of lifeless, loveless shadows. "Sex in the head", D H Lawrence called it – "an awful disease and difficult to cure once it has got a hold". Another poet, Yeats, referred to it thus: "We have fed the heart on fantasies; the heart's made brutal by the fare".

Nothing but ill can come from such a grounding – and don't let any experts tell you differently. Particularly since, if they have the sort of obsession with sex that has enabled them to pass themselves off as "experts" in the first place, they are likely to be suffering from "sex in the head" themselves.

Which takes us back to the first remarks in this chapter and to the important fact that parents have a responsibility to pass on to their children their own standards and beliefs. They should do this regardless of the claims and posturings of strangers in the guise of experts who offer something radically and disturbingly different without being responsible for the results.

So much material that is mind-bendingly cruel and obscene is available to young people today, and I think it more important to keep them away from it than to stop them smoking. Things that damage the individual's body may be bad but they are far less significant than those evil things which poison the mind and deform relationships with other people. Yet our culture condemns the one and condones the other.

You are, after all, working alongside your children's own instincts about what is good and bad, healthy and unhealthy when you warn them about the danger of pornography. They understand perfectly, if you talk to them about it, that you want them to keep vile images and a cruel, rapacious attitude towards women in particular out of their minds; just as you want them to keep junk food and dangerous chemicals out of their bodies.

Fortunately, when they are young and sensitive, they too know what is bad in itself as well as bad for them and they are impressed (and I suspect relieved) at your commitment and concern. They may not tell you so for years, but they often do interpret, quite rightly, their parents' "funny little ways" as an expression of love and are grateful for it.

A handicapped child

I decided to include a chapter on having a handicapped child in the family, simply because one of mine is handicapped and it is something that, although it affects only a few people, interests many more. It is also something that is bound to cross the minds of prospective parents, and many mothers wonder what they would do if it ever happened to them. It is worth passing on our experience if only because, if we had known at the time what we know now, we would not have shed the tears we did then.

Everyone is always so gloomy about handicapped children, as if having a handicapped child were the very worst thing that could ever happen to you. I certainly know from my own experience that we were far more miserable at times because of the attitude people took to our child than we ever were because of what he was like.

True, one has to get used to the sheer shock of having a child who is classed as "handicapped" but, before long, one comes to realise that being a parent is not for the weak-kneed in any case. It is a tough job that absolutely requires you to mature and "cope". The parents of children who are delinquent, drug-takers or depressives also suffer, and so do parents who lose a healthy child through disease or accident. In short, one realises that having a child makes one uniquely vulnerable to suffering – regardless of whether that child is handicapped or not.

There have been many occasions when I have felt far more sorry for the parents of a chronically sick or difficult child than I ever felt for us. One can only accept the fact that the price of loving anyone is that, along with all the joy and pleasure, we are likely to spend at least some time grieving or worrying over them. It is the old maxim, expressed by William Faulkner: "Between grief and nothing, I choose grief". Unless one accepts that philosophy, one would be foolish ever to have children or even to fall in love.

Our second child was born, fortunately, at home, and the midwife told me right away that he was a mongol. I was too stunned to speak for a while, and just lay there trying to remember what mongols were! Chubby little people with funny eyes was all the information I could summon up, and the midwife, mistaking the silence, said, "Never mind, dear, you can always put him in a home if his vacant eyes get you down".

My husband, who had just brought us both a cup of tea, looked at the tiny bundle she had deposited in the cradle and said, "Well, son, it looks like we are the only friends you've got!"

All through the night we lay on the bed trying to come to terms with what had happened that evening. Our inexperienced minds, so unaccustomed to grief, longed to shake off the nightmare and return to a comfortable reality. But it could not be done. The doctor came and went and so did another midwife; both, I now realise, practising that belief of the medical profession that it is a bad thing to encourage what may be groundless hope.

Finally, after a couple of hours' sleep, I awoke to find another midwife, a mountain of a woman, peering into the cradle. She had just called in on her rounds, but I do believe that a particularly sensible angel sent her, because the sunshine of her personality put a different perspective on everything. "You have got a little 'natural' ", she said, with such love and warmth. "He'll be the joy of your life, don't you worry. You will never regret having him when you realise what he was sent to give".

She was the only one, of all the professionals, who ever got it right. That all you need to make you pick up any burden cheerfully is to feel that the sorrow will pass and that there is some purpose in it.

He was a lovely little baby right from the start and seemed to us to be particularly good just to make up for the anguish he had caused us. I fed him myself with no difficulty, and he slept through the night from 10 days old. His eyes were never dull or vacant and I searched his little face in vain for signs of what everyone felt was such a tragedy.

By one of those strokes of good fortune that often seem to happen when you need them most, I heard Rex Brinkworth on the radio a few weeks later, talking about mongol babies and his "Down's Baby Centre" at Birmingham. A letter to him at the BBC produced a reply by return, and then some instruction sheets about how to systematically exercise and stimulate the baby at every stage of his development.

More important even than these valuable instructions were his own positive and helpful ideas on the subject. It was so nice to get away from the doleful tones of the inexperienced professionals whose one resource was to commiserate.

Here was the father of a child like ours, and yet he was not lying slumped in his chair with his face on his shoulder, talking about a life-long burden being his lot. He was vigorous, funny and obviously enjoying a life in which his little daughter's progress and achievements were major factors.

He even confessed to having had the same feeling of contrariness as we had had, when the doctor told him that his daughter "would never be anything but a vegetable". He felt the doctor was not qualified to make such a prophecy and that, whatever she was, he was going to do all he could to help his daughter develop her potential. He introduced us to the term "Down's Syndrome", which is the correct name for what is commonly known as mongolism. We used the term assiduously when Matthew was small, probably because we did not like the association of "Attila the Hun and the Mongol Hordes" with our baby! However, after a couple of years, I discovered that there were several people of my acquaintance who had taken my use of the correct name to mean that Matthew was not only a little mongol but he had Down's disease as well! After that, I felt it was more important to ensure that people understood what one was talking about and so use the two names as appropriate.

I have mentioned before that many professionals who work with handicapped children seem to believe that the worst thing you can infect parents with is hope – just in case it is false hope. However, this ignores the fact that many of the plans and ideas we have for all our children look, in retrospect, to have been rather optimistic and as redundant as the violins and drum-kits mouldering away with the looms and chemistry sets in the attic. By the time such hopes have not been realised, we have moved on to other aspirations that are also situated somewhere in a bright future. Hope is the means by which people find the enthusiasm to travel many otherwise dull roads, and we can never seriously regret the efforts we make towards things, even when they fail.

Mr Brinkworth lives and breathes hope and, because of that, his advice on helping handicapped children is very valuable. Particularly appropriate to us was the fact that his programme of things to do with the child was written on plain, foolscap sheets that you simply worked through. At that time, we were not quite up to seeing pages of photographs of handicapped children and wondering which one ours would be like.

In time one comes to recognise and put in affectionate context the different faces of handicap and not to feel frightened or put off by any of them. One grows in understanding with experience, but it takes time to learn to love and respect your child for what he is without too much reference to the future.

Matthew sat up at nine months, well bolstered with cushions to stop him keeling over. He walked at two and a half, having spent more than a year getting about on his bottom with an amazing leg movement that he should have patented.

There was really nothing different about his progress except that it was slower than other children's. He was always loving and cheerful, responsive and obedient, and he had a very normal sense of his own dignity and pride in achieving what he knew he could do.

He has always loved music and stories, games, walks and outings. His tape recorder is his favourite possession, and company his greatest pleasure. He was then as he is now, small, slight and healthy, and I never did anything different for him.

This last may come as a surprise to those who believe that being handicapped makes a child entirely different from other children. In fact, of course, their similarities are far greater than their differences, and they are first and foremost *children*.

Although I do not know a great deal about other kinds of handicap, I do know that Down's Syndrome people are the largest single category of the mentally handicapped, comprising nearly a third of the total. To me, unless they have other illnesses, they do not present a very great problem at all. It is far more likely to be their parents who are the problem, or perhaps the attitude of the society into which they are born.

They are just what they are, and they neither threaten nor attack anybody. They give out a lot and, if they have the chance, many of them can contribute their labour to simpler jobs in the same way as anyone else. They are, for example, nothing like as difficult a problem as the habitual criminal, and yet our society has a hysterical attitude to them, which can turn, in a moment, to outright rejection.

Parents, on the other hand, may well be in the position of having created most of the behavioural problems associated with their child by being over-indulgent. Like so many parents of spoilt children, they feel that they have done their best for the child because they have had to work so hard to give him everything he wanted. The resulting ungovernable little beast is looked on with pity and further indulgence by friends and relations, who wrongly think that the behaviour is because of the handicap rather than the spoiling.

It is natural for parents to want to indulge a child whom they feel has got difficulties, but really it does them no good. Indeed the resulting bad behaviour cuts the child off from other people in exactly the same way that it does with other ordinary children.

One advantage of having a large family is that everything is not left to the parents to decide. The children themselves play an unconscious part in correcting imbalances and providing stimulus where it is needed. Certainly, in Matthew's case, he has been extremely lucky to have several bossy, opinionated, caring peers to help and push him along. Being the eldest boy, they expect a lot of him, and I doubt whether we would have discovered just how much he could actually do if it were not for them setting the pace and keeping him up to it.

They make very few allowances for him except, perhaps, in the case of teasing, where he has not got the repartee to equal theirs. He has, however, developed a lofty way of dealing with their cheeky remarks and will say, "Don't be stupid, will you", in the tones of a bored aesthete.

In many instances his brothers and sisters had a direct motive for getting him to learn to do things, because it relieved them of a job. In consequence of this he has learnt to pull his weight and is a responsible boy, far too sensible to allow a baby to climb the stairs or fall off a chair. He takes care of himself more or less completely and can do a very good job at cleaning and tidying a room. Despite the fact that he has an IQ of 70 or under, he enjoys very much the same things as the other children. They all love ballet, music, theatre, and the cinema, so whatever the points on an IQ scale mean, you obviously do not need all that many of them to enable you to enjoy life.

It is very interesting how different the attitude of our children to Matthew is compared to that of my husband and me. We initially had a shock to get over, but they have never known a time without him. Consequently, they did not have any expectations for him to fulfil, and so cannot really see him as handicapped.

They get quite a few treats because of him, through gestures of kindness being offered by local organisations. A free afternoon at the fair, for example, or tickets for the circus, or pantomime for handicapped children and their families; there is never any shortage of volunteers to "ride shotgun" with him on such occasions. After one such enjoyable outing, Sophie asked in conspiratorial tones, "What happens if they ever find out that Matty is not *really* handicapped?"

One of the unexpectedly pleasant things about having a handicapped child that you could never anticipate at the outset is the extent to which, because of him, you encounter the best side of people.

So many of those who work for or with the handicapped have a full-hearted tenderness for others that one just does not meet in many areas of life. I do not really know what it is, but something about the vulnerability of the handicapped seems to personify all sorts of inner weaknesses and incompletenesses which one does not normally see, but which we all feel in some form or other. It is as if they are publicly enacting a heroic struggle with adversity which is an example to everyone, and many people feel the significance of it.

It is a source of great inspiration and happiness to be so often reminded of the love in people; how much we need each other in order to express some things and how even the weakest have their part to play.

The question implicit in the remark of my old midwife, "when you realise what he was sent to give", she never answered. Perhaps she knew that there was no one answer and that people come to understand it each in their own way. Certainly it is an eventful journey that each parent makes from the time when they first have their handicapped child.

Initially, of course, it is your pride that takes the biggest knock. You do not realise, until you have a less-than-perfect baby, just how much the child is an extension of yourself; how important it is to you that in appearance, behaviour and potential it is along predictable lines and in keeping with your image.

It takes a good deal of self-adjustment to accept that this child will not be part of the armoury with which you face the world. It will not just be part of "that nice family" or "those lovely children". You will have to go deeper if ever you are to understand what it is all about. Even when you do, it is difficult to express. There is an inscription at the start of *The End of the Affair* by Graham Greene, which runs: "Man has places in his heart which do not yet exist and into them enters suffering that they may have existence". The development of these places in the heart provides the fountainhead of all our civilised values and no society which accepts and cares for its weaker members can ever fall completely into barbarism.

The family is a microcosm of a democratic society and within it the members learn many useful lessons from knowing someone who is handicapped. They learn that life-enhancing virtues, like courage, cheerfulness, sympathy and goodwill, can be present in a person who does not have much of the intelligence by which we set so much store.

*   *   *

Matthew is now a young adult. Apart from a short period after we moved house, all his school life was happily spent in mainstream education as part of a small unit within a school, with its own specialist teacher. They joined the other children for every kind of non-academic subject and activity and Matty benefited enormously from being always surrounded by the pace and standards of normal behaviour.

Looking back on it now, I think that he really had the best of both worlds because, being always with ordinary children, he did not acquire an image of himself as being primarily "handicapped". This confidence and sense of being much like everybody else has stood him in good stead ever since. He knows that he is slow and that there are many things he cannot do, but so what? He accepts it as another person accepts that they have big ears or a tuneless voice; just part of the basic equipment you were given.

On the other hand, being in a small group of special-needs children in the school meant that he was not swamped by children of greater ability in academic subjects. There were two other Down's children in the group of six and three with other disabilities. Slow learners have a keen appreciation of one another's efforts and progress which is quite genuine and unforced because they share the same degree of difficulty. So they do not suffer from the mute demoralisation that can sometimes occur when they are in a normal classroom with other children who are academically on another plane to them. In drama, music and painting they could genuinely hold their own with the other children, and were bursting with exuberance and confidence because of their lack of self-consciousness in these pursuits.

At sixteen he went on to Further Education College, to begin the process of learning a trade in a course designed for slow learners like himself. The course lasted three years and the end of it coincided with his brother William's "year off" before going to university. They spent a good part of it touring the Middle East on foot, tandem and camel. They even climbed to the top of Mount Sinai, which William said was no mean feat, and spent the night there watching the sun go down and then rise in the morning. For them it was the high point of the trip, literally and figuratively, and Willy felt sure that it was the first time that a Down's person had climbed to the spot where God gave the Ten Commandments to Moses.

When he returned, a bronzed and seasoned traveller, he found a job through an agency which helps disabled youngsters with employment, and has been working full-time ever since in the kitchen of a Cambridge college. He loves it, and earns more than a hundred pounds a week, paying not only his taxes but his own pension scheme and private medical insurance. Not bad for a person whom some people do not believe can have a "life worth living".

Most of his workmates came to his 21st birthday party, as well as everyone else we could think of who had helped him on his way. When it came down to counting, there were so many. Bless them all; I could never guess exactly what motivated their kindness, but, whatever it was, it is surely one of the reasons why children like Matthew are put on this earth in the first place.

Older children

This is the only chapter of *Good Children* that has been more or less completely re-written since the second edition came out in 1990. At that time, the whole country was gripped by what might happen as a result of AIDS. Even the government thought that we were all "at risk" and a leaflet was put through the door of every house in the UK, telling people that that they would have to be extra careful, regardless of whether they were old, in stable marriages, crippled by illness or decisively celibate, like a nun.

It was absolutely obligatory to mention it in speaking to young people then, since my own children were agog with what was going to happen next. So I spoke about the disease and how the ancient moralities of chastity and fidelity were likely to be some comfort and protection in such a context. The problem then was that no-one was sure whether the disease could be spread by more means than simply sexual contact. I went to a parents meeting at one son's school, where the Headmaster told parents that the joint use of musical instruments might have to be discontinued, and that almost anything used by more than one person might prove to be a danger. My daughter at the Further Education College received a leaflet warning that "deep kissing" might be a source of infection if they had any lesions in the mouth, or gums that occasionally bled.

Thankfully, these fears turned out to be groundless and the disease has confined itself mainly to those who have had contact with the three known high-risk groups which were, and are, homosexuals, hard-drug users and those who contracted the disease abroad, usually in sub-Saharan Africa. Recent figures from the Public Health Authority show that the majority of AIDS cases in Britain are restricted to these groups.

So the debate has moved on, but the problem of infection resulting from what Nature plainly does not like or accept – that is, promiscuous behaviour – has not. We are engaging in a major war with nature if we think we can change this just because of our new technology. In the past, people accepted the limitations of nature because they did not want to be diseased or infertile. Religious people would say that they observed God's hand in the laws of nature and based their morality on them. Agnostics would say that people made the best of a bad job and invented devices like religion and romance to make youthful abstinence more palatable.

Whatever your point of view, the fact remains that, for all our cleverness, 35% of all sexually transmitted diseases are incurable, and are spreading at an alarming rate, particularly amongst the young. In response to this, the authorities are clutching at straws and urging ever-more sexually explicit sex-education upon children, including an obsessive concentration on the almost magical powers of condoms. Consider this highlighted information contained in a booklet issued by Health Authorities up and down the country:

"FACT: Only condoms provide all-in-one protection against pregnancy and sexually transmitted infections, including HIV."

This statement is just not true and, what is more, it seems to me to be deliberately misleading. What does "all-in-one" mean here? That it doesn't come in three pieces that need to be assembled? That there are other devices that have footwear and gloves to accompany them? It is meaningless but it gives an impression of being dependable and risk-free. That is what young people would make of it. That is what many of them *do* make of it.

The matter is therefore urgent and I decided, in this chapter, to follow the agenda that is most often set for me by young people. Since my own children have grown up, I spend a lot of my time giving talks to sixth-form groups and college students; sometimes following up on a recent article or a television programme I have done. Regardless of the title of any of my talks, we always seem to end up talking about what concerns them most – and that is their frightful ignorance about the "facts of life". They are propagandised in many of their encounters with "Health professionals" – but they are seldom told the truth about another reality that awaits them far more certainly than the ideal of sexual freedom they have been promised.

Many of these groups are quite large, two or three hundred young people, and someone will usually start the questions with something like, "Why do you think so many girls get pregnant then?" There is usually laughter at this point, and I turn the question round:

"Why do *you* think they do? Is it because they have never been told the facts of life, or do you think they didn't know about condoms?" There is usually quite a thoughtful answer then, because the person knows that his peers are checking the reply against their own experience.

"There's lots of reasons", they say. "They might not have done it right, (laughter); they might have been drunk or the condom, you know, like, fell off".

"So you do think they would have been using a condom then?"

"Yes, of course; everybody knows about safe sex, don't they? And you don't just suddenly have sex; do you? – unless you're a bit of a slapper. I mean, you know it's going to happen, she's probably your girlfriend at the time, so you take a condom".

"So what goes wrong? Do you think they are just inexperienced and put it on their head by mistake? Haven't they been shown what to do with it?"

"Yeah, they know what to do with it. Blimey! We've had so many lessons about that . . . they'd be stupid if they didn't." (more laughter) "All right, you tell us why, *you think,* they get pregnant then".

"Well, I would have thought it might have something to do with the failure rate of condoms, don't you?"

That is the first bombshell! They often howl with laughter at that point and shout out, "Haven't you ever heard, *it's safe!*" They invariably turn to look at whichever teacher is responsible for "Health Education" at this point – if she is in the hall – and this lady generally nods sagely in agreement.

So I point out that even the contraceptive manufacturers concede that there is a failure rate for their products in practice and that it is about 15% for married couples and a good deal higher for people of their age. "Some researchers have found it to be as high as 40%, but let us take a lower figure and say that it is about 20%. That still means that if there were one hundred girls in this room who all used condoms at all times, about twenty of them would get pregnant. In other words, there is a one-in-five chance of getting pregnant – roughly the same odds as Russian Roulette!" This is a useful analogy because anyone can see that you would not shoot yourself every time. Other things have to be factored in when calculating how soon you *would* shoot yourself.

The young people are incredulous and disbelieving. At one talk, they even appealed to the teacher to refute me but, since I always carry the relevant statistics in a folder with me, she didn't argue and I was interested in her obviously sincere answer. She said that she was well aware that condoms had a failure rate but didn't over-stress it. Since young people could not be restrained from "having sex", it was her responsibility to see that they at least lessened their chance of getting pregnant by using a condom.

It is a common point of view; but doesn't one usually mention the risk factors inherent in any dangerous activity, and then leave the participants to make up their own minds about whether it is worth it? The fact is, most young people don't know about the dangers of what is often a fairly experimental, rather than a deeply felt, foray into sexual experience.

At a meeting at Cambridge University, I asked a group, "What do you think 'Safer Sex' means? Safer than what?" Their answer was so interesting that I have asked it many times since and the result is always the same. About half of any group think it means, "safer than nothing at all". The other half thinks it means, "safer than safe". As they often say, "You were safe before, but this one is even safer than that! Man, are you safe now!"

I tell them that the answer is, of course, safer than nothing – which is exactly what condoms are. Then I ask them why they think this product is labelled in this way and, after thinking about it – usually for the first time – they say that probably it is because they could be sued if they claimed a thing was "Safe" when, in practice, it wasn't.

I agree with them and do not believe that it is just happy chance that the condom industry has stumbled upon a form of words that is ambiguous to most young people. It encourages them to use it, in the belief that they are, indeed, "safe".

This pattern of misleading young people – for their own benefit, supposedly – has extended, even more crucially, into the way the government health authorities are handling information about sexually transmitted diseases. (STDs) The same booklet that I mentioned before, contains the information that "many young people do not know about STDs". Having said that, the booklet then says nothing whatever about most of them – except for two things. They have the following, prominently highlighted information: "Factoid: Up to one in fourteen young people have an STD called chlamydia, often it shows no symptoms but, if left untreated it can leave 10–15% of sufferers infertile. Always use a condom."

Now doesn't that suggest that if they use a condom, they won't catch it? I think it does, otherwise why mention condoms at all? But they know this is untrue and the fact is often mentioned, in muted tones lest it offend anyone, in the medical pages of newspapers. In fact, "one in fourteen" young people sounds quite small, doesn't it? It doesn't sound as alarming as "hundreds of thousands" anyway.

The most definitive study we have was conducted by the prestigious and dependable National Institute for Health in the United States, which published a report in July 2001 in which it reviewed all the published literature on the subject of condom effectiveness to date. It found that, "there is no clear evidence that condoms reduce the risk of *most sexually transmitted diseases, including gonorrhoea and chlamydia*". (my italics)

Just think about that for a minute will you? There is nothing to show that condoms reduce the risk of catching an STD. So why are we telling teenagers

– who are, according to government figures, the most vulnerable to acute STD infection, that they will be "safe" if they use one? Young people obviously fear STDs yet, instead of telling teenagers about them plainly and with some of the graphic precision that they bestow on other areas of sex education, the Health Authorities seem to be doing everything they can to leave them in ignorance.

Here is another pearl of wisdom from an ubiquitous advice booklet, issued in this case by Cornwall and the Isles of Scilly. "Many young people today are not fully aware of the risks of HIV and other sexually transmitted infections. *If you are worried that you may have been in contact with a sexually transmitted disease through unprotected sex . . . then you can go for free, confidential, anonymous tests at the Dept. of Medicine.*"

In what other field, dear readers, will you be warned about a dangerous activity, by being told where you go to get help *after* you've got hurt, but nothing else. They just avoid the issue.

They certainly are not telling them that condoms offer little protection against STDs, nor that they are a growing menace. I have not seen one booklet which mentions that STD infections doubled from 1990 to 1999 and that, in that year, they stood at 1,170,000 and are still rising in great leaps. In other words, they give young people no idea of what their chances are of catching a disease by means of sexual activity.

I recently gave a talk to teenagers and their parents in a small town in a sparsely populated part of the country. The figures I had obtained about STDs there, showed that they had more than 400 cases of Human Papilloma Virus in just 3 small towns in the area. This is the most common STD in Britain and is incurable. It produces unsightly warts in the genital area. It can respond to long and uncomfortable treatment, but the virus is there for life. The American National Institute for Health Report said that it was responsible for 98% of cervical cancers in women. The report also said that condoms have *"no impact"* on the spread of this disease, which can thus be passed on at every sexual encounter, with or without a condom.

This is startling, isn't it? And yet no mention is made of this – let alone the implications of it, in the booklet or in the information produced by the local Health Authority. They simply ignore it as if it will go away rather than go on spreading.

The reason I think this is wrong in itself and potentially disastrous is that, at about the time the original AIDS "scare" was filling the media, some people began to voice concern about what was happening in Africa. We had a medical student living with us at the time and he did his probationary year in Africa so we got it from the horse's mouth, so to speak. He told us that medical opinion there believed that *if* the spread of AIDS followed the level of STDs in Africa, there would be an epidemic of the disease in that country. Well it did, and now they have catastrophic numbers of people sick and dying of the disease, and still no solution in sight.

The reason for the original speculation was that it was always suspected that the spread of HIV was related to venereal infections which cause lesions in the reproductive organs and it is these which facilitate the entry of the HIV virus into the bodies of heterosexual men and women, who are outside the usual risk groups. Once it got into the heterosexual population, then it would spread like wild-fire. Any country, therefore, ought to be taking a great deal of notice of any increase in STDs, particularly in young people.

In the UK we know that the official "risk" of catching HIV is 1%, but that is because it is not yet widespread in the general population. The American National Institute figures for condom efficiency against HIV infection is 87%; that is, they have a 13% failure rate in laboratory conditions and if the condoms are in perfect condition. Even so, it seems to me to be wicked to promote, in Africa, the use of something that will cause 13 people to die out of every 100 who use it during sex with an infected person.

However, in practice, the situation is even worse. A study among prostitutes in Kenya found a 33% infection rate amongst those who always used a condom[1]. This is roughly the same as that found amongst HIV-infected young people by Dr Margaret Obola in the Cottolenga hospital. "The disbelief and shock in the reaction of young people when they are told they have AIDS is heartbreaking; – 'But it was SAFE sex', they tell me", she said.

Quite so; but we are ensuring the same habitual ignorance here and, furthermore, we are perpetuating the myth that young people are incapable of restraining themselves in sexual matters, even if they were to know that it might be fatal.

One final reference to the American Report – that seems to have sunk without trace here – is that the President of the Medical Institute for Sexual Health, who contributed to the Report, said this: "All future sex education programmes must reflect the information that is consistent with the Report's findings, otherwise the programme should be considered *medically inaccurate*."

Well, I've asked the question so I might as well try and answer it. Why do the relevant authorities mislead young people in this way? The answer is, I think, because they have a certain way of looking at things. So many of those who work in the area of sex-education come from the Family Planning Association and its off-shoots and they are, and I don't suppose they would disagree, "contraceptive-minded".

As a matter of fact, they also have what some would see as a financial interest in *not* discouraging sex. The Brook Advisory Centres were set up by the FPA in 1964 and were, at first, funded by the FPA. Some of the joint directors of these companies then formed a separate company in 1972, Family Planning Sales Ltd. The interesting thing is that the *surplus profits* from this company are covenanted back to the FPA. In other words, the FPA does have a financial interest in the selling of condoms. In any other, similarly controversial area – such as smoking or drugs – the media are hot-foot after any conflict of interest. Why is it only in this area that they have gone in for a "willing suspension of disbelief"?

However, it is seldom simply commerce that has the power to drive along a great band-wagon like that of liberal sex. That is where ideology comes in. After all, what are the logical consequences of having to accept that casual sex – of the sort we see all the time on the television and in every other medium – is actually dangerous to health in a serious way?

The "chattering classes" have given their unconditional support to the sexual revolution that is producing so many young, hapless casualties. These are often the same people who scan tins of vegetables to see if there are minute traces of something that might knock ten minutes off their life expectancy; and who complain if someone lights a cigarette in the same building as themselves. How can they face having their most cherished life-style option branded as "dangerous"; even "deadly"?

It would be the death of all their dearest fantasies and would involve having to concede that religion had grasped more of the truth about real life than they had. In short, they just cannot bring themselves to say that we may have to accept that the price of sexual freedom is too high; for the individual and for society.

Fortunately for our survival as a society, however, there is a growing movement that does not have this horror of nature's way. They are young, enthusiastic, and they are the driving force behind the programmes of abstinence education that are currently making such progress in the USA. They have reclaimed chastity for the young as their birthright and they are not a bit embarrassed about it.

Various "spokespersons" for the sex-education lobby have, predictably, tried to rubbish this movement, even though they seem to know nothing whatever about it. But distinguished commentators like Melanie Phillips[2] have taken the trouble to go to America and to judge for themselves how it is working and what is the effect. It has been, for the most part, a well-documented, thumping success and their government is now vigorously supporting it, even financially. It has been effective in lowering illegitimacy and disease, sometimes dramatically, whilst in many cases increasing the educational achievement of the most disadvantaged pupils well beyond what most people expected.

These abstinence programmes work because they are imaginative, new and exceptionally well thought out. One of the many initiatives used in this new way of educating children in abstinence rather than sex, is the use of young people, usually students, who go round schools to demonstrate a positive view of chastity. They use sketches and quick-fire games to demonstrate typical situations in which young people find themselves. They are often very funny, as when they demonstrate "ten ways of saying No"; and reproduce some of the cheesy "chat-up" lines that are current. They are also touching in their personal experiences of being used and discarded, and of the fear and worry that blights the lives of those who have got caught up in an often unwanted sexual merry-go-round.

They are not embarrassed by virginity but treat it as an asset that demonstrates personal autonomy. It is a part of their youth and they want to treat it as special. The ensuing freedom from anxiety is shown to be worth more than keeping up with the sexual Joneses of their peer group.

Until I saw one such group, "Challenge" from Canada[3], giving their presentation on a tour of schools in England this year, I would not have believed it possible to be so up-beat on the subject. In fact, the contrast with the typical sex-education professional could not be more marked. For a start, they are unpaid and do it because they believe in it enough to subsidise their trips out of their own pockets. They are also at the start of their lives and full of the energy and "can-do" optimism that often goes with that. They also do not use crudity as a means of establishing their credentials to talk on this subject. None of the young people in their audiences needs cringe with embarrassment at graphic descriptions and crude, mechanical scenarios. We can only hope and pray that abstinence education faces down its critics and becomes the norm here too.

In fact when you think about it, in the context of what young people are really like, what appeal is there in the idea of having a penis in the middle of a board game; or huge black and white drawings of genitalia to pass around a mixed group in order to teach them – what? How to be crude, how to overcome any feelings of delicacy or modesty? It associates the subject entirely with lust, ugliness, and – oh, yes, "Don't forget to buy those condoms now, will you?" That's always the end result of any lesson – don't forget the product it is promoting.

No wonder some young people have rebelled against it, and no wonder their current dreary, middle-aged sex-educators – who try so hard to appear "with it" – fear having the whole thing taken out of their hands and given back to this new generation, whose lives are still in front of them.

Since this chapter follows on from the one about sex-education, you may well ask whether it alters anything I said there. The answer is, no, but there is a rider. Children today sometimes need to be protected from those in authority. It was only in January, 2002 that public pressure from parents forced the Scottish authorities to withdraw sex-education material from their schools that was quite plainly obscene. People who talk graphic sex to children in any context outside the family, should be treated with suspicion and may be suffering from paedophilic tendencies. Parents would be wise, therefore to protest forcefully if any material comes into the classroom that would be seen as abusive if it were presented to their children in any other context.

Actually, if one considers the effect of the government actually deciding to promote chastity in schools, one can see how enormous the changes would have to be and how total the shift of emphasis. When looked at from that point of view, one can clearly see just how propagandistic current sex education is. Good heavens; can you imagine trying to discourage football hooliganism by showing films and photos of young men battling with one another? Close-ups and examples of the weapons they use and scenarios of how a fight might start; the "cool" armour they could don in the heat of battle; all bullet-proof, of course. Plus, of course, absolutely no mention of either the nature or the number of the injuries inflicted, the cost to society and, certainly no interviews with casualties. Would *anybody* seriously think this was the way to do it?

The root of the problem is that the people who are currently in charge of sex education are not basically in favour of young people abstaining from sex. In its Annual Report 2001 the Brook Advisory Centres describe their mission as: "Equipping young people to enjoy their sexuality without harm". Unfortunately, they cannot deliver the one without the other, except by chance.

If only that "mission statement" had read, "Helping young people to enjoy their *youth* without harm", how much more suitable it would have been. But then, it wouldn't have included the obligatory reference to the "equipment" they provide and the clinic would probably have no reason to exist.

My own family is Christian, so chastity before marriage, and fidelity within it, have always been accepted as normal and natural, despite the odd backsliding relation or two. Neither does it seem to have been too onerous. In many respects the young actually have less need of sexual intercourse to animate their relationships than almost any other adult age group. With their extravagant emotions and acute, obsessive perceptions they have a feast of enjoyment from one another without the necessity of fornication. Of course sexual attraction is the basis of a lot of their behaviour, but how that attraction is deployed in their own interests is crucial. I do believe that they need to beware of being *seduced* by their culture into abandoning their natural inhibitions, which are, after all, there to protect them – their feelings, their self-respect and their health, now and in the future.

The problem is that romance is a crusading ideal and not just a sloppy emotion. It is a serious philosophy which believes in the seminal value of passion, properly harnessed for the good of all. As such it needs to be passionately and seriously expressed, as it was when it first swept Europe in the thirteenth century, by troubadours travelling from place to place spreading its message and gaining converts to a new, much more interesting way of seeing the relationship between the sexes, that was called "romance".

Their eloquence started a romantic tradition that lasted until the beginning of the permissive age and the marketing of sex as a commodity that has reduced almost every kind of relationship to a simply sexual one.

If the will is there, it could be rescued by that modern equivalent of the troubadour – the mass media – and restored to its former importance. As a tradition, it has never lost its appeal to the imagination; and romance, both in the classics *and* in popular culture, is as sought after today as ever it was.

The return of an ideal of unconsummated sex in youth might have another fundamental effect apart from its role in limiting the spread of misery and disease. It could help reduce the number of divorces by returning the *courtship behaviour* of young people to something akin to its true nature.

The 1960s were a great period of social change and many old laws and traditional practices were abandoned in the name of progress and improvement. Many of them have produced results that are quite contrary to what the advocates for change originally envisaged, and nowadays we can hardly remember the reasoning behind some of their theories.

One such perverse improvement was the idea that if a couple lived together before getting married, then there would be fewer mistakes in choosing a permanent mate and, hence, less divorce. Now however, official statistics confirm that marriages contracted after a couple have lived together first, break up more quickly and more often than other marriages. The intriguing question is why; and the answer is, I believe, relevant to the foregoing remarks about romance.

Romance is a sort of courtship ritual transformed into an art. The art, though highly artificial, nevertheless only disguises a process that is even found in some animal behaviour, where it serves a strictly practical purpose associated with the survival of the species. Its function in those animals where it features, is largely to provide *time* for the male to demonstrate his skills as a provider of food and shelter and his devotion and fortitude as a protector of the female and her young. The female needs the time to decide whether he fits her instinctive criteria. She then consents to mating and, a pattern of co-operation having been established, they stay together to raise the young.

This *natural* need for a relatively uncommitted period of assessment between people, to establish intimacy and knowledge before they get married, is what we have ignored in our recent culture. We have failed to grasp that the function of courtship is to establish compatibility before the commitment of marriage. We haven't noticed that consummated sex is important after marriage for precisely the same reason that it is counter-productive before it.

After marriage, a new sexual relationship is important because it has the power to blind the parties to the inevitable difficulties of adjustment to a situation where, however desired it is, there is a certain loss of independence and "sovereignty". It cements a relationship in the face of those aspects of it which at first do not work very well and it makes bearable the sometimes painful process of two people growing together. "Making love" is a literal description of what takes place in a fully consummated act, and the time for that is *after* deciding, more coolly, that you are genuinely compatible.

This blinding power of sex which is such a help within marriage is, however, disastrous when you are *choosing* a mate. You do not want it to cloud your judgement and disguise major differences when you are getting to know someone. You cannot afford to be swept away in a sea of emotion at a time when you should be assessing more deliberately those qualities of character and temperament you will need to last a lifetime.

When talking about marriage rather than casual affairs, sexual intercourse has always been described as a consummation. That is, the culmination of a ritual and not just part of a journey. This ritual, which we call romance, most likely served as a vehicle for minimising mistakes at a time when men and women were becoming more free to choose their mate than they had been previously when the choice had been made largely by their families.

In departing from the time-honoured practice of a sexually unconsummated period of courtship, we have bequeathed to our children an unworkable strategy for choosing a mate that has caused immense suffering to couples and to their children, who lose one of the people they love most in the world when their parents separate.

There is another aspect of cohabitation that I would not have thought of myself if friends of my children had not mentioned it to me. It concerns the difficulty that some couples have – particularly the young men, I must say – in deciding whether to turn cohabitation into marriage. They live together, so they share all the advantages of the married state; they have intimacy, companionship and mutual help. They are also free. Mentally, psychologically and legally, they can "walk out" at any time without too much hassle.

When they come to contemplate getting married, therefore, the married state is at a disadvantage. It offers no more than cohabitation and it is loaded with responsibilities and expectations. I have on several occasions comforted a weeping girl who has spent several years living with a young man until she felt ready to settle down and have children. Then she found, to her great grief, that he was not willing to marry her. In the shock of discovering that this person whom she felt was her friend and soul-mate could treat her so badly, she left the home they shared, only to hear a short time later that he had married someone else.

This is quite a common scenario and a heart-breaking one, particularly if it is the girl who is ditched. She has a much shorter time in which to have her family before nature makes it difficult to conceive, and no amount of "equal opportunities" has altered the fact that a man in his late thirties is still considered quite eligible, whilst a woman is usually not.

Maybe it is the unacknowledged recognition of this fact that makes women, if they are sensible, take marriage very seriously. Let us just say then, that it does not take "true love" to make a man live with you – which is probably why only 4% of cohabitees stay together for even ten years, with or without children. Marriage is the test and, despite any impression to the contrary, a big majority of them do last. [4]

---

[1] N Nzila, M Laga, M Kivuvu, R Ryder: *Evaluation of condom utilization . . . among prostitutes in Kinshasa*, 1989.

[2] *America's Social Revolution* by Melanie Phillips, Civitas, 2001.

[3] The "Challenge" team can be contacted by e-mail at: challengeteam@comnet.ca.

[4] "Less than four per cent of cohabitations last for ten years or more." [*Cohabitation in Great Britain*, Ermisch & Francesconi, Institute for Social and Economic Research, 1995].

The child within the home

The mother, the child and the home go together as a natural entity. In whatever dim and distant past a woman first began to rearrange the rocks in a particular cave, to put down soft grasses for a bed and make primeval curtains to keep out draughts, she must have done it because she was, at least temporarily, immobilised by having a baby or children to look after.

Husbands could be off hunting with the boys, collecting food or doing a spot of weapons training down at the clearing, but the wives, when they had children, would be preoccupied with the struggle to keep them alive and healthy and to educate them in the language and ways of the tribe.

Both had a big job on their hands, and neither one would be less important than the other. No doubt the husband valued what his wife was doing to keep him in domestic sufficiency and to raise and educate his children; just as she must have appreciated the food and protection he gave her.

Even looking back down the dark tunnel of time, it still seems a pretty good arrangement and, give or take a few variations, it remains with us today. The reason it has lasted so long, men and women being the selfish, happiness-seeking creatures that they are, must be because it works reasonably well for all concerned and better than many of the alternatives which may have been tried.

Probably the most difficult part of the arrangement has always been the relationship between the two adults in the family, and that must be why their choosing one another and their coming together always seems to have been surrounded by ritual and ceremony. Such a time-consuming device as courtship gives both parties a chance to assess one another, and become acquainted without irrevocable commitment – even creatures as relatively uncomplicated as ducks and bob-tailed wombats seem to need it.

The coming of children, on the other hand, never seems to have worried parents unduly. Problems associated with having a new baby were always confined to the material ability of the family to cope, and the health of the mother. Apart from that, the child himself was not seen as a problem or his coming as something one needed training to undertake. Untold generations of parents, often with very large families themselves, passed on to their children and their grandchildren the various tricks and techniques that might help to calm a fretful baby or curb a wild boy and, for the rest, people absorbed laterally, from the people around them, how to rear children with the minimum of stress and trouble.

Come the 1950s and '60s, and a whole new breed of people expert in the rearing of children arose to give advice that was backed with the testimonial of science. They had medical degrees and psychology degrees and it did not seem to matter to anyone that these do not indicate any real knowledge or understanding of children at close quarters or in natural surroundings. What is more, very few of them could claim to have brought up even one small family.

The most amazing series of crazy theories followed upon their general acceptance as experts in the field and are still to be found in those areas where common sense and practicality never penetrate.

A few years ago, I went to a prestigious conference where an educational psychologist cited in his talk the problems experienced by a young mother who had an active four-year-old who kept opening the front door and running off down the road. She liked to rest after lunch, being eight months pregnant, and this daily excitement was getting her down.

The psychologist told his numbed audience that he had worked out with the mother what he called a "successful strategy" for dealing with the situation. Was it to give the child a most frightful roasting? Or a good smack? Or something to do? Or even to bolt the door . . . ?

No. He told the mother that she must dash out of the house after the child and immediately go into the road where the child would not look for her. Then she must *crawl on her hands and knees* – I swear this is the gospel truth – on the outside of parked cars until the child reached a road junction where she would stop and look round for her mother.

If the unfortunate woman had not already been run over or arrested, she was to remain hidden there until the child began to get really frightened and bewildered, and then she was to heave herself up and come forward as a saviour.

Someone asked the speaker whether this programme had been accepted and if it had worked and was told brightly that, yes, it had, and that the woman had said it worked marvellously.

One can only say "Ha! Ha!", and speculate that what the woman had really done was to put a lock on the door in the hope of keeping the child in and the psychologist out.

Fortunately for our sanity as a nation, most ordinary people did not take much notice of the books or the experts on the subject of how to bring up their children, and so remained relatively unaffected by them, except that their children would often be taught or otherwise supervised by people who *had* read them, and therefore made a terrible dog's dinner of quite simple disciplinary matters. However, by a curious freak of chance which only a satirist could adequately describe, the women who most readily accepted a philosophy that made them slaves to their children's every whim and wish, were very often the same women who stressed most urgently their right not to have to remain in the home – or indeed the room – with those same children, but demanded the right to go out to work and leave them to someone else.

And who can blame them? Compared to looking after the spoilt little monsters that the philosophy created, a day spent resurfacing a motorway would indeed appear a soft option!

Is it my imagination or do we seem to hear less of both these conflicting philosophies nowadays? Do we instead hear that gentle, far-off sound of a tide, or a worm, turning? I do hope so, because both these ideas contributed to the current low status of the housewife: the child-centred philosophy, because it meant, in fact if not in theory, that one had to be a "mug" to do it; the "farming-out" one, because it placed a great deal of emphasis upon escaping from the role of mother, and so made the job seem a waste of anybody's time.

Certainly many of the people who absorbed and accepted this new approach as a basis for bringing up their children had a very hard time of it with their families. There seem to be fewer of them about, now that the first wave of children brought up in this way has passed into adolescence and adulthood, but it is still possible to find oneself in company where the mother is interrupted, shouted at, shaken and even kicked by a child trying to get what he wants. Somehow, however, it is less socially acceptable now than it was a few years ago. Perhaps that is because it is more obvious that such behaviour does not suddenly cease just because the child reaches adolescence, but continues in the forms now so familiar to us from "lager louts", "hooligans" and "yahoos" of every class and background.

It is a much healthier and happier state for the family to be in, if everybody, and that includes the mother in particular, has a reasonably easy time. One knows that there is a certain amount of physical work to do looking after children, but the most important aspect of the relationship is the living and learning atmosphere in which the child grows up.

If the mother consciously aims at making the child accommodating to her and to others, by being undemanding and considerate, she will be doing everyone a big favour.

For the adults in the family there will be the freedom to do things and to go places, with the child sharing the experience but not seeking the limelight and so dominating the scene.

For the child, it means that he will not be excluded from interesting occasions because his bad behaviour means that he is always left behind. He can always be around whatever is going on: playing on the floor while the grown-ups are discussing or making things; curled up on a knee when music is being made; participating in interesting events; being talked to and played with by different, friendly people. Instead of always being confined to a child's place somewhere well away, he can go anywhere with his parents and watch the world unfolding, from their shadow and protection.

What you want to avoid like the plague is the situation which playschool so often reveals, where the child behaves perfectly well with everyone *but* his mother.

Perhaps the women running a playschool are a little older and more experienced with children. They will have given the child a firm and kindly framework in which to operate which he will have accepted, as children invariably do, cheerfully and co-operatively. Then his mother will come to collect him and, even as he is getting into his coat, his "home" manner will be returning – aggressive, demanding, discontented. It is an infallible sign that the mother has not given him enough genuine discipline, and he tramples all over her for it, making himself miserable in the process.

This, then, is the heart of the traditional approach to bringing up children, and it embodies two inextricably linked ideas. Number One is that your children must fit into the family and into the world – rather than the other way round. Number Two is that the job of child rearing is absorbing, rewarding and absolutely essential for any orderly society to have as its basis.

From both of these propositions one would conclude that the job is not something that one should decide lightly to leave to someone else. Indeed, I would like to suggest that the case for or against delegating this duty to a crèche or baby-minder may be as simply put as the case for bottle-feeding compared to breast-feeding. If your circumstances are such that you have no choice then, of course, you must. Otherwise, don't!

There is not a shadow of doubt about it; babies under the age of two and a half or three years old hate leaving their mothers for the very simple reason that they love them and need them. Just how much they need them becomes, with experience, obvious to all mothers observing their children over a period of time. It is perhaps not so obvious how comparatively badly babies get on without their mothers because the mothers concerned are unaware of it – not being there themselves. The baby-minder is hardly going to draw attention to it and do herself out of a job.

My own experience as a child-minder lasted for over four years and started when the youngest, Oliver, was a few months old. All the other children had started school and he was alone at home, so it seemed a good idea to get in a few more to liven things up. We also needed the money!

It was a simple matter to register with the social services (which you are required to do by law) and our house was duly inspected. They were not looking for a high standard of comfort, nor for a particularly "enlightened" atmosphere, but simply for a very ordinary home with no obvious dangers like unguarded fires, exposed points or piranha fish in the garden.

After that they referred children to me and played no part in whom I agreed to take, the hours involved or the money paid. The children who came were a complete cross-section, from well-off homes where the mother was a lecturer, to single-parent families where the mother was struggling to make a living and care for the child.

At first I was enthusiastic and open-minded about what I was doing, and would happily take a baby for the whole day if that was what the mother wanted. Mostly though, they came for only half days, odd days or intermittent whole days.

It was only after a couple of years' practice and several experiences of taking a baby full-time that I realised fully why this length of time was wrong for the child and, to a lesser extent, for his mother.

The loving relationship between mother and child is the context in which early learning takes place most easily and naturally. Children have an urge to learn, which flowers when they are happy and relaxed and withers when they are not. Cast your mind back to how little children love to play with older ones and to tag around after them trying to keep up and improve their performance. And think how closed and aloof those same children are if the company is alien or unfamiliar to them, or when they are not happy.

It is one of the pleasant surprises of parenthood that your child actually likes you – it is much harder to understand than why they should love you. They are constantly acting and reacting for you, imitating you, showing you things, being interested in you, and generally wallowing in the relationship. They learn so much in this way that one can only speculate what the effects will be if a relationship is missing.

Looking after another person's child, even when you are fond of one another, is a quieter, less intense affair altogether. When you know how babies *should* be, and what they are like when they are thriving and developing at full capacity, you also see clearly when they are functioning well below par.

The mother and child relationship is a truly passionate one, with very strong feelings on both sides. Because of this strong love, nothing you do together really seems a waste of time or even requires very much effort. You may look back and think how awful it was when you had to get up in the middle of the night because of coughs or sickness, but at the time you did it without much bother because the child's discomfort was yours too.

In the same way, the endless feeding and cleaning routines of babyhood that the mother has, and the endless learning that the baby has, are just incidents in a relationship that has got more to do with new love than anything else.

It is not a sexual love, of course, but it is a physical one, and the amount of kissing and cuddling that goes on is comparable to what we put into adult relationships. Surely the point of it all is that you do much more for each other and make more effort with everything when you love in this way. The baby learns in order to come closer to the mother, and she unconsciously teaches him by all the manifestations of her love: playing, singing, being amused with antics and impressed by progress; taking time over washing, feeding and dressing; making him repeat things for her because the expression is so delightful.

Even a humble walk to the park to sit in the sun and feed the birds becomes especially enjoyable when it is done with someone you love. It is reminiscent of the hours spent watching a boyfriend greasing a filthy motorbike in a freezing cold garage – it makes you remember the power of new love to make ordinary things special.

This experience of new love is the same for a baby as it is for a young person or adult – and as it is for the mother if she gives it a chance to develop, rather than curtailing it by going back to work and leaving her child.

It is a time when the emotions have a chance to grow and mature because they have been awakened by love. Care, concern, interest, subtlety, sympathy; they all arise first out of this love and, if exercised freely and without anxiety, settle happily into the child's personality.

It does seem that we ignore this early love and its educative power over our emotions perhaps because, by the time we *could* express it, we have forgotten its details.

However, I feel sure that one day even the psychologists will stumble onto what people have always known – that a happy and fulfilled "love affair" with his mother sets a confident and cheerful child upon the road to growing up.

This is a kind of committed love that no baby-minder, however affectionate, can give to any child other than her own, because it is a temporary affair – and, anyway, she does it primarily for money. For this reason, I eventually decided not to accept any more babies to look after for longer than four hours a day. If I was approached by a mother who wanted day-long care for her baby, I would take the bull by the horns and tell her honestly what I thought. It was an embarrassing and presumptuous thing to do, and yet it was surprising how often it turned out to be not necessity that made mothers seek full-time work, but a belief, fostered by a half-baked media opinion, that they were doing the right thing for themselves and that the baby would not be affected.

There were of course some women who genuinely needed the money of a full-time job in order to pay their bills, but, by thinking over imaginatively the possible alternatives, we were often able to work out a different strategy; part-time work plus a lodger, for example. On one occasion, a woman whose husband had left her with a young child, decided that she was not being very imaginative in planning to do exactly what her husband would have done in the same circumstances. So she decided instead to become a baby-minder herself and to add to her family circle rather than cutting herself off from it.

One certainly finds out sooner or later in life that there is invariably more than one way of solving any problem. The trick is to give it enough thought and to ask around until you find out what others have done and then to work out a balancing act whereby the needs of all the affected parties are met.

New ways of earning a living are springing up all over the place in response to a shrinking labour market. Certainly, as far as women are concerned, a remarkable revolution is well underway that can only help them, particularly if they are bringing up a child on their own. I read in a magazine recently that one small cul-de-sac in London contained: a woman who had a cattery in her garden, which cared for the neighbourhood cats for weekends and holidays; two women who made patch-work for the rag-trade; a woman who grew herbs on a small balcony for herbal cosmetics that someone else made, and which were then sold by a co-operative of women who had a market stall. And finally there was a woman who made a good living doing fashion knitting on a machine.

In my own neighbourhood, the last few years have seen dramatic innovations amongst friends and neighbours. One buys old furniture from the local auction, which she strips, cleans and sells through the local paper. Another does dressmaking to order, and yet another does hairdressing at home. Two friends have branched out into boarding students during term time, and another makes computerised language games for use in the teaching of English.

Surely all this activity is the most fruitful change that has occurred on the women's labour market since the time when the "go and get yourself a proper job" ethic first affected people many generations ago. As was remarked of women during the '20s and '30s: "They said they would not be dictated to, and went and got themselves jobs as shorthand typists".

Since then, countless women have taken the same, often thorny, path into jobs that existed primarily to satisfy the working requirements of men, and with few, if any, concessions made to the fact that they also had a home to run and children to look after.

About crèches and day nurseries I can say very little, except that they are totally unsuitable for very young children. A baby is not yet a "group person", and has very little interest in other children of the same age. In the absence of the mother it is another adult that they seek, someone to cling to, someone to form a relationship with, to help to make up for the loss of the mother. This is generally impossible in the context of any institution, however small.

The question of whether the mother's role can be taken over entirely by the father is rather different. There is no doubt that, by being a permanent part of the family, the father is in a better position to do so than almost anyone else. He knows and loves the child in the same committed way that the woman does, and most fathers do a splendid job in the support, interest and affection they invest in the little group that is nurturing the growing child. However it must be said that men seldom show much aptitude or skill at those subtle and profound things which a baby needs, and which most mothers supply naturally.

In the first place, of course, men have never been able to produce the primary means of feeding the baby themselves, which is, in a way, symbolic of all the other things they cannot produce. They also cannot produce femaleness, and I would guess that babies of both sexes need to be surrounded by it. For example, babies need, and women produce, endless talk expressing calm, appreciation, concern, interest, disapproval and so on. This verbal knitting imprints itself on the child's mind, containing expressions of female values and emotions, sounds of the language, the structure of sentences, nuances of meaning and the music produced by question forms and exclamations.

This is vital for a child's progress both emotionally and intellectually, and women produce it naturally – some would say for most of their lives – although men usually do not. Watching a man change a baby's nappy or preparing the food is often like watching a film with the soundtrack switched off. Usually, it is unnaturally quiet and free from the remorseless babble that mother and baby keep up together.

Then again, the things mothers talk about when they are with other mothers revolve to a large extent around things connected with children. They are simple and direct things to do with feeding, illnesses, dangers, milestones, problems and anecdotes which women need to discuss in order to share experience and increase their knowledge.

The child hears these things chewed over many times as he plays, and his own comprehension improves as he listens to the talk. The subject matter is, after all, connected to his own experience, so he is drawn into understanding rather than being excluded from it. It is so personal and people-centred that he is given a little lesson every time a neighbour comes in for a cup of tea; listening, as G K Chesterton said, to "women, with their great hearts and love of little things".

If my husband is anything to go by, men feel very differently when a friend comes to call while they are doing the baby-minding. All they want to do then is to get away from the subject of children and to get on to something which is nearer to their commonly expressed interests, such as their work, sport or politics, from which a little child can deduce nothing.

I really do not think that my husband was unusual in this. I can honestly say that of all the men we have known who, like us, have boxed and coxed with their children at times, not one has liked to talk about the minutiae of babies and life in general in the familiar, comfortable way that women do, and which is such an education to their children: even if, like my husband, they have enjoyed doing the job itself.

Vive la différence, I say; it is obviously for a purpose, and I would hazard a guess that it has to do with a child's needing to absorb the feminine qualities of gentleness, sympathy, communicativeness and warmth before the more masculine ones which follow. In any case, does it not denigrate both the innate skills of motherhood and the abilities of the mother, to insist that anyone else either could or should take over part of her responsibilities? No one, for example, would dream of suggesting that the wife of a successful businessman had a duty to help and counsel her husband throughout the day. Any such suggestion would be taken to mean that the man was inept or that the job was beneath anyone's dignity to do full-time.

Naturally it is nice, and only fair, if fathers lend a hand with the chores when they see that it is needed, which will include looking after the children. But, in saying that, one is really saying no more than that rigid job-demarcation lines have no place in a loving home, and that people who care for one another, help one another.

It does not seem to me to be necessary to go to great lengths in defining the "role" of the father, since men and women have always been able to adapt themselves to changing work patterns and social conditions in a way that is mutually agreeable. Because men and women love one another and always have done, then whatever arrangements they arrive at in any particular age are a compromise between the power that men have, because of their physical strength and earning power and the overriding influence that women have – both as mothers of their children and as wives.

In the past, as now, some men have been more involved with their children than others simply because some men *like* children more than others do, and find it easier to relate to them. Given the variations produced by these differences of temperament, the traditional role of the father can still be seen to embody no more and no less than what they have to give to the relationship.

Unquestionably, fathers are important to their children and probably for the quite simple reason that a child needs an intimate (and that means a loving) experience of both sexes if he is ever to get on successfully with either.

Fathers spent a lot more time with their children, on the land and in home-based crafts and workshops, in pre-industrial Europe; even as they do in "under-developed" countries today. But the relationship is always recognisably the same, however much the circumstances change. It is not remote, but neither is it as close as that which exists between the mother and child from the time when the mother produces the child from out of herself and only gradually nurtures him for an independent life.

This nurturing towards independence is the fulfilment of a promise implicit in the idea of motherhood. We tend to make very heavy weather of this commitment today but, in truth, all childhood passes very quickly, leaving most women with twenty or thirty years more to pursue a career or a regular job. It is a daunting prospect, and one which leaves me feeling very glad that my sex does not keep me chained to a concept of work that describes a straight path from youth to age with no natural pauses or digressions.

Bringing up a child can be a very pleasant occupation by any standard, and it follows a reassuringly ancient pattern of parental involvement with the growth and education of children. It is an aberration on the part of our culture at present to see this kind of arrangement as slavery for the woman and a denial of her personal development. It is anything she chooses to make of it, and nothing at all will be lost by women accepting that they have as much power over their own lives within the home as they do within the confines of a job.

I have long harboured the suspicion that the irrational denigration of the role of housewife, which characterises our culture at the moment, arises primarily because it is a job that is genuinely classless. In a very materialistic society like ours, we like to be able to put a price on people, and that is very difficult when a woman merely says, on a questionnaire or at a party, that she is a housewife. In fact, the modern world has many horrible, boring, cold, uncomfortable, lonely pointless and pernicious jobs for people to do – but being a housewife is not one of them. On the contrary, it is rewarding and necessary work with far more potential than is commonly recognised.

Perhaps it is because educationalists have not given sufficient emphasis to the different circumstances of girls after they leave school that so little is done to prepare them for a productive and fulfilling home life. This is an unforgivable oversight when one considers that more than 90 per cent of girls say they want to get married and have children and so will be almost certain to spend at least some of their most active and creative years in a domestic environment. They will thus have more time and opportunity than most for planning and carrying out paid work at home, but they need information about this and plenty of working models.

One of the improvements that an enlightened headteacher could make would be to invite knowledgeable and experienced housewives into the school to demonstrate their skills. How the style and atmosphere of the rather dull home economics class would improve if it comprised such subjects as bread and roll making; the brewing of ale and wine from common fruits and flowers; how to make cosmetics, face creams and shampoos; and how to prepare and administer herbal remedies and "medicinal compounds", most efficacious in every way, as the song says!

Educationally, all these subjects have impeccable credentials. They involve practical knowledge of nature and natural science, nutrition and chemistry. They could not be said to be beneath the intelligence of even the ablest girls and they are likely to be useful in later life whatever the girl chooses to do. In this they are directly comparable to boys learning woodwork at very academic public schools, even though they will probably all go on to university, because it is a skill that almost every man, regardless of his job, will find himself being asked to exercise at some time in his life.

On the academic side, one comes across the same bias in favour of a bland, unisex curriculum that ends up giving boys what they need more than girls. The assumption, again, is that everyone is going to have a career or a job, and none are going to need to know how to adapt it to a home-centred life.

A more realistic approach for girls contemplating marriage and motherhood would surely be to include some talks and advice on how to adapt a typical career so that it could be continued from home or on a part-time basis. There are likewise many options or specialities even within a typical career, such as teaching or nursing, which lend themselves to a more flexible working life, and these need to be identified and discussed. For example, speech therapy and language teaching are two professions where it is relatively easy to arrange flexible hours, and where the work is increasingly done in the practitioner's home.

It would also be very useful if, alongside all the sociology and liberal studies, they could learn how to set up and run a co-operative, so at least they would be able to buy foodstuffs and materials cheaply with other housewives for their own use and for any enterprise they might want to start. They could also learn how to register a small business, and what typical outlets there would be for new producers. Girls are far more likely to be their own bosses, at least for a time, than boys, and there should be some element in the education system which takes account of this fact and prepares them for it.

Only when our society starts to prepare girls for the option of motherhood and domesticity with the same care that it prepares boys to be workers and managers will the public image of the housewife improve. It is a state of personal and cultural maturity to accept that there is more to "having a baby" than just giving birth to him. Having gone in for the experience, one has a responsibility to do the job properly, just as one would if it were animals and not children that one had chosen to raise!

In these pages I have tried to show what *properly* means, and I hope you will agree there is nothing difficult about child rearing so long as one is prepared to give it the one basic requirement – time. Not a lifetime, nor even a decade, but a few happy, vital, irreplaceable years that enable you to set a stalwart and integrated individual on the road to his or her future. As that little figure moves off down the road, the increasing distance making him smaller even as he grows bigger, the mother can truly feel that she gave him everything she had when it was needed.

"The hand that rocks the cradle, cradles the rock" as S J Perleman said. Yes, it certainly creates a kind of strength to rear a family successfully, but it is a strength that is inimitably a woman's. Not a pale imitation of the kind of strength that orders people around at work or claws its way to the top in business. It is a strength that arises out of love and care, and the awesome, undervalued responsibility of creating and preparing another human being for life. It has been woman's strength since time began and scarcely a person alive has not felt its effect. Like all true strength it did not need to be shouted about, and this present age – unused to the modesty of the really first-rate – has tended to forget that it even exists, preferring instead the lesser status conferred by a "real" job.

One thing is certain, however: homes are ruled by women in a way that few other places ever are, and by someone who is essentially a free agent. The combination of freedom and autonomy has created the type of domesticity which has nurtured in the family the individualism and love of freedom that has characterised our culture down the ages.

We should not allow ourselves to forget that, nor what it means to assume that which Mr Micawber called "the lofty character of wife" and the irreplaceable skills and responsibilities of motherhood.

Just goes on growing! The latest addition: Riffen and Kathleen's baby, Felix.

Some common questions answered

1. How important is choice to a child? Should a child be given a choice about everything, or is this a waste of time?
I don't think choice is important to a child at all unless you make it so by setting up an elaborate system of alternatives for the questions, say, of food, clothing or activities. Children eat what you give them and wear and do roughly what you suggest unless and until they really discover something they do not like; and then, at least, you have a genuine emotion to go on.

Being obliged to have an opinion about things which don't matter is a very poor training for a child and, being entirely concerned with material considerations, encourages a greediness and preoccupation with the importance of mere things which will probably influence them all their lives.

Furthermore, as one can easily see from children who have been brought up in this way, freedom of choice is often used to dominate and manipulate the parents. Refusing food because it is on the wrong coloured plate or asking for food that is not currently being prepared are very common examples of the way in which children lead their parents a merry dance while, at the same time, becoming thoroughly inconsiderate and calculating.

It is better to be quite free of these inconsequential details as a child and to be unencumbered by thoughts of how much better you might have done if you had chosen otherwise. In any case, is there not something morally damaging in giving even a child the idea that a prominent part of life is composed of making choices between a range of luxurious options? It somehow separates them from those people who often have no choice in life and gives them the idea that, for them at least, the rules are different.

2. What do you do to stop a little child being jealous of a new baby?
The answer to this is really quite simple. A new baby does not know if he is being complimented and admired or not. A toddler does. Therefore, lavish all the interest and the compliments on the child who understands whilst being perfectly normal with the baby. It must be very tiresome, as a toddler, to be constantly ignored in favour of an inert heap that never says or does anything interesting and one understands why young children get irritated at too many displays of familial and neighbourly attention towards the infant. When it is

your own toddler who is a bit jealous of a new baby that too is easy to understand. The feeding and cleaning routines do take up a considerable amount of the mother's time and it is not only toddlers who mourn the passing of a more leisured age. Involving the child in some of the childcare is an important way of making him feel that his seniority – which at this time appears to be the reason he misses out on some love and attention – can be capitalised on. He can wash the baby, for example, and sing to him; keep him amused by talking to him and be made to feel very superior by taking those disgusting nappies away and putting them in the bin!

3. What do you do with a child who talks all the time?

Do more or less what the rest of the world will do with him. That is, listen and answer for as long as you are able and then tell him to be quiet because you've had enough now! You do not want the difference between home life and the outside world to become too startling. If it does, the child is in for a nasty series of shocks once he moves away from the home environment, and that can make him feel ill at ease and anxious.

4. Do you think you should insist on table manners?

It is not really a question of insisting. If you *teach* children reasonable table manners, they will use them at least for most of the time. Most children whom we call "bad-mannered" in fact have no manners. It is their misfortune that, even if they wanted to behave better because people don't seem to like them the way they are, they do not know *how*. Of course, all children forget their manners from time to time; they would not be children if they didn't. But it is a great source of confidence to them, that they do know how to behave when necessary.

5. What do you do with a child who does not need much sleep?

We had two children like that. After a few hours of sleep they would be wide awake and ready for a game and a little drink. What a drag! Neither my husband nor I have much largesse or good humour at night, so we simply put some toys at the end of the cot, left the curtains open in the room so that there was some light, and put a lidded cup with orange juice on the cupboard next to the child. It was a perfectly regular routine that worked well because the children knew from the earliest that we would not come and play with them. We had to open the curtains and put the toys in place after the child was asleep and just before we went to bed so that the temptation to play was not there to begin with.

6. How would you deal with a situation where you suddenly find that you have developed an antipathy towards one of your children?
One of the most difficult things to deal with in our lives is irrational emotion. This is no doubt why all institutions which deal intimately with people's lives – like the family, the Church and the law – have developed rules and dogmas which provide balance and continuity in the face of the ups and downs of human feelings and moods.

In fact, though the subject is deep, the answer is short; you do your duty and you love the child without it seeing that the love is forced. What else can you do in all fairness? You keep uppermost in your mind the realisation of what pain and confusion it would cause a child who has done nothing consciously to repel you, if you consistently showed him your dislike or feelings of aversion. It will help to heave you over the occasions when you are tempted by both.

Above all, it is important to try and shake off becoming absorbed by your antipathy. It is wrong and self-indulgent to think that one is ever free to hurt the innocent just because we happen to have taken a dislike to them.

There is also the opposite problem of naturally preferring one child to the others in a family. My experience is that *all* children think you are doing this at one time or another but that all believe in the end that you love them the same. The same criteria apply here as in the former case because one must be guided by principles of fairness and justice within a family if one is ever to pass these qualities on. As a matter of fact, even the act of pretending to feel certain emotions helps towards bringing them back to life and one is almost certain to find that it is just a passing phase rather than a lasting one.

7. My husband comes home from his job bored with work and eager to play with the children. I finish the day bored with children and eager to talk about work. Is there any way we can reconcile these two extremes?
Wonderful! Why don't you just hand the children over to him for an hour or so and put your feet up with a good book. After they are in bed, you can have a good chat about work and so forth.

8. If another person's child behaves badly in your home, how do you deal with him?
Well the first thing to be said is that children behave according to your rules in your house regardless of what might be tolerated in their own homes. I cannot really see the point of complaining to a child's mother about his behaviour in your house. If you don't like it, why not just say so and deal with the problem

on the spot? A firm and hearty telling-off will probably do the trick as long as you make it very clear that you mean what you say.

I think you will find that children who are allowed to behave badly in their own homes become very attached to outsiders who make them behave better – like teachers, cub or brownie leaders or other children's ferocious mums! What happens is that they are obliged to be nicer and less selfish and so they feel better because it is a miserable business being unpleasant. They associate this overall feeling of well-being with the person who has been instrumental in achieving it and value the power that they have to make them behave, and so feel, better.

9. Do you think that it is ever too late to change a "spoilt" child into a normal, pleasant one?
No; I do not think it is ever too late with children, or indeed with human-beings, to change and improve. It is just that some methods, like bitter experience for instance, are rather unpleasant and unnecessary ways of learning what you might otherwise have learnt with less pain if someone had taken the trouble to teach you.

If one day the parents of a really spoilt child wake up and realise that he is a selfish little beast and no earthly help to anyone, they could quite easily change the circumstances that brought the situation about and go for something more disciplined.

However, most parents do not see the light in quite that way. What more often happens is that they realise how unpleasant their child is and will look to the schools to overcome his social disabilities. Some parents even pay vast sums to send a spoilt child to particularly tough expensive schools as a way of doing their "dirty work" for them! Similarly, many people will remember a few years ago when there was National Service, and the tales of various selfish, conceited mother's boys who were straightened out by a system that would not take "no" for an answer and made everyone muck in and lend a hand regardless of whether they wanted to or not. Indeed, the transformation was often little short of miraculous and it was all because of a discipline that was both impersonal and rigorous. It cut through class, privilege, talent and even intelligence so that the classroom swot who had always been the apple of everybody's eye – except his contemporaries – had to clean the lavatories just like everyone else. A very good short novel on the subject is Rudyard Kipling's *Captains Courageous* (Oxford University Press).

10. What happens if mother says one thing and father says another? Who should the child be taught to obey?

This is something that parents have to work out between themselves independently of the child. A lot of children will try the old trick of trotting from one parent to the other in order to get less of a dusty answer – and not telling that they have already been turned down once. A shrewd parent, knowing these crafty little subterfuges, will always ask if they have already asked the other person and, if so, what answer did they get.

By and large, parents handle such questions as relate to their own sphere of activity or interest. Thus any questions about normal domestic problems will be directed towards mum who is likely to know most of the background while dad will receive referrals from what the full-time administrator cannot answer. It is a bad idea for either parent to undermine the other by giving counter-orders; you could not run any enterprise on the basis of two bosses who are free to contradict each other, so it pays to get these things sorted out beforehand.

11. Should you pay children to do housework?

What a horrible idea! Are you at the same time going to give them a bill every week for their food and shelter? The family is based on love, kinship and mutual help; paying children to participate in that relationship changes it into a much lesser thing.

However, offering an occasional "fee" for specific, perhaps rather tedious jobs seems to me to give them a chance to experience what earning is all about. My children sometimes asked me for a "fee-paying" job because they needed the money to buy something they particularly wanted or needed, and then I would find something like cleaning the windows or clearing out the shed for them to do. It is not a bad thing to get them used to the idea that your labour is something you can sell in order to get things that you want.

12. How much housework do you think it is fair to ask a child to do?

You must be careful not to simply use your children to do all the jobs that you find a bore; that really would not be fair. The only criterion I use is that they look after their own things: making their beds, tidying their room; washing and ironing some of their own clothes once they reach, say, fourteen. Apart from that, I would expect them to do some things that were of more collective benefit such as laying the table for meals and clearing away afterwards. They do a lot of shopping for me which is considered an enjoyable soft option and they join in a weekly "purge" on stairs and landings which gets it all out of the way for a week. Of course, on any special occasion that produces extra work for the parents, they would join in to help; but then so would any co-operative person in any collective situation. One is only helping them to acquire the habits of a good spouse, neighbour and citizen in showing them how to lend a hand and, particularly, to be quick about it.

13. Do you think that all children should be treated the same way in a family or do you think there is a natural "pecking" order?
Children should all be treated according to the same *principles* within a family – justice, honesty, trust for example – but while there is a difference of age, maturity and responsibility, you will never treat them all the same. For instance, there has to be some compensation for the responsibility that the older children carry for the younger ones whenever they are on their own. They have to be able to feel that, as they are expected to act more sensibly they are given more privileges because of it – they are able to stay up later, receive more pocket money and generally enjoy a little bit more freedom of choice consonant with their position.

There is a further aspect to this pecking order. If you do not want the older child to get too severe and coercive with the younger ones, then the latter must be taught to respect their older brothers and sisters. You cannot expect any child to have to keep order when they are temporarily left in charge of younger ones, if those little ones are allowed to be as cheeky as they like when they feel like it. Children have their dignity too and if others are allowed to attack it too much they will resort to violence in its defence.

14. Do you make girls do boys' jobs and vice-versa?
The basic point is that all young people should be able to do a reasonable job in looking after themselves and being useful in other, fairly normal situations. For example, I would expect any boy to be able to make a cup of tea and cook a simple meal for more than one person simply because he may need to do it one day and would be at a disadvantage if he didn't know how. In the same way girls should know how to do practical things like fixing the plugs on their electrical equipment and mending punctures. Both sexes should know how to keep their environment clean and hygienic and how to look after their clothes. However, the fact remains that there are some jobs that girls detest doing and some jobs that boys find just as repellent. For example, most of the boys that I have known detest ironing and would never do it if it was up to them. Even clean and orderly young men will wear un-ironed clothes quite happily for most of the time and

only iron for special occasions or certain clothes. Most girls, on the other hand, detest jobs which involve them getting very dirty; particularly things to do with machinery. So, once the simple business of learning all the basic skills is over, you will very likely find that young people evolve their own "division of labour" and will very sensibly "trade in" those jobs which they cannot bear to do, with someone else who feels the same about some other task. Thus, my son will ask his sister to take in his trousers on her machine in return for him fixing her gears next time they go wrong. It may of course end up looking very conventional and "sex-stereotyped", but there we are! One might have guessed that people always were following a genuine bent when they were doing what society expected of them.

15. Do you think it makes much difference to a child to be the first or the last in the family?

I don't suppose it alters their inherited characteristics like basic intelligence and talent; but I am sure that it must alter quite a lot of other things. Starting at the bottom: the youngest always develops a strong personality as a means of survival because without it he would quite simply be swamped. They learn to assert themselves very early on and also how to exploit the fact that they are the youngest, so that concessions are made for them. This means that they learn to be crafty little beggars with quite a good knowledge of people's personalities. They are often very quick on the uptake because of the amount of talk they have absorbed that was near enough in content and expression to be fully accessible to them and so useful; and they have numerous good and bad examples to learn from by way of their older siblings.

The oldest child has both the best and the worst time of it. On the plus side, he enjoys his parents' individual attention for quite a while before any others come along to take up some of his space. He also has, for many years, the superiority in physical and mental matters. On the debit side, older children are always being challenged by the younger ones once a certain age is reached, and have to come to terms with the fear of being overtaken or equalled in some spheres where habit has made them always feel superior. Between these two extremes lie many variations. None of them are entirely negative or entirely positive; like all things in life, one makes the most of what one has.

16. Is it a good thing for children to keep pets?

Yes; animals are important to children and that is as it should be. After all, they share our world and greatly enhance it. A child looking after animals on a daily basis discovers far more about their beauty and habits than could ever be achieved by simply looking at them from afar. I think it probably satisfies some ancient husbanding instinct to be responsible for another creature, and they must always be taught how to do the job properly so as never to leave the animal in hunger or discomfort.

17. Is there such a thing as a naturally bad-tempered child?

No, I don't think so. If you have a child who is often bad-tempered, it is almost certainly related to the way he has been brought up. Getting in a bad temper is only one of a whole range of possible responses to events and it is a particularly unsociable one. If it has become a habit then that is because no one has shown the child any alternative and has not deterred the negative response. Indeed, it probably means that the child has been led to believe that it is a fruitful response by the fact that it has often produced exactly what he was after: his parents have given him what he wanted, or jumped about trying to please or satisfy him. So he will go on using bad temper as a response to certain events and, eventually, to many more things as well until it becomes an automatic reaction to discomfort – real or imagined.

Children who erupt quickly with temper when they are thwarted are really only people with a volatile nature. If they are quickly and firmly told that it does not help to get cross they will calm down and try again. It is important for parents to exercise an influence over displays of bad temper, for it can make all the difference to how a basic temperament is projected onto the world.

18 What do you do if your child prefers one parent to another?

Nothing; it will almost certainly pass or at least change. The important thing to remember is that children *love* their parents; they do not necessarily *like* them all the time. Of course it is nice if they do and very often this is the case because they share many characteristics shaped by family and environment as well as the ones they have inherited. But it does not necessarily follow that the child will feel the same interest or affinity with both parents equally. Love goes on unchanged at a much deeper level than the surface transactions of family life, so it is important not to take any inequality of interest or affection too personally. One thing is for sure; you cannot force a child to feel differently by insisting upon it. If it really mattered to you that you were thought to be boring, for example, you could try to be different, but on the whole it is better to take the attitude "Flipping kids!" and wait until it passes.

19. Would you maintain that parents have a right to dictate who their children's friends are?

If one could put this question another way, it would make the answer sound more reasonable. Do you think that parents should acknowledge that their children's friends will influence them in some way, with that influence not always being for the best? Most people would agree that this was the case, and if so I would say that parents have not only the right, but also the duty, to protect their young children from harm from whatever quarter.

There has been an occasion in the past when I have asked a teacher at school, for example, to move my child from sitting next to a silly and disruptive friend. I would certainly extend that to say that any dishonest, bullying, seedy or overly powerful child should be quietly sent packing without too much preamble or ado. One just doesn't take chances with one's children where they can be avoided and there are always plenty of alternative friends for both parties anyway.

When the children grow a little older, the main thing in your favour regarding the suitability of their friends is the fact that your children are likely to share your values, though not necessarily your opinions, about the things that really matter. Thus, for example, though they might have friends whose clothing you do not like, or whose attitudes or ideas you do not share, they would be very unlikely to become attached to someone who was disgustingly cruel to animals or who liked harassing or assaulting old people.

It must be said, however, that children will only respect their parents' beliefs if they first respect their parents! By the time you have waded through this book you will know what I mean by this and how to set about achieving it.

The really important point is that, unless "parental authority" has been a feature throughout your child's life you stand no chance at all of being able to impose it in adolescence, simply because the issues are now very serious. The parents who have been unable to control the tantrums of a four-year-old will not be able to do any better when that child is fourteen and wants his own way, regardless of the cost.

It may be a terribly unfashionable thing to say, but there need to be some things that a child would not *dare* to do because of parental reaction. They need to know, and to have a healthy respect for, the righteous fury that any excursion into drug-taking or shop-lifting would provoke in their parents. This predictable strength of feeling in the adults, if part of a close and loving relationship, is usually accepted by children as an indication of love and care.

20. Is it better to have a very free attitude in the home to nudity or should one encourage modesty?

You may think that this is a simple matter of form; but let me assure you it goes deeper than that. Modesty is *natural* to human beings and any attempt to do away with it is *fashion* working and not *freedom*. Left to themselves, children become modest at about four to seven years old. A privacy closes around them that protects something, and I have never quite understood what exactly it is.

Parents who believe vehemently in nudity will often put enormous pressure upon their children to feel the same way by laughing at the "unnatural" behaviour of others and equating it with fear or prudishness. The child cannot question these things and so has to suffer the parents' nudity although, deep down, it might be deeply offensive and even frightening to them. We know such a child and remember with pity when he came to stay with us and my children discovered that he had his pyjamas on under his jeans and would not reveal so much as an ankle in getting up or going to bed. He was a complete neurotic at twelve years old, which is just about the time you would normally expect things to start easing up a bit. The excessive modesty gives way to a greater or lesser extent as the child becomes older, but never completely disappears. It is always there at vulnerable moments to represent a feeling of privacy and wholeness.

21. I was recently told that it is possible to correct sticking-out ears by taping them back. Do you know if this is true?

I'm glad to say it is! Since many members of my family have protruding ears, it is a matter of some interest to us too – particularly when one of us is expecting a baby. I wish I had known before that this defect can be easily corrected. Writing in the *British Journal of Plastic Surgery* in 1994, Mr D T Gault of Mount Vernon Hospital said that soon after birth the cartilage of the ears is very malleable. Not only "bat ears" but also other types of ear deformity can be easily corrected by taping the ears back in the first six months. I would certainly have done so if I had known, and saved a bit of heartache.

22. What would you say when someone asks you at a social gathering, "And what do you do?"

I reply, "Guess!" and then encourage them to blunder about asking, for example: Are you in management? – Yes. Creative? – Yes. Forward-planning? – Yes. Financial? – Yes. Practical? – Yes. Any physical aspect? – Yes. A boss? – Yes.

You get the picture? If you are positive and proud about it, it's a great chance to promote the many skills inherent in being a wife and mother. Never apologise for it, and people won't be so inclined to be indifferent or patronising.

Appendices

Appendix One: Smacking

As soon as I saw the report *Spare the Rod?* issued by the Family Research Council of the USA in 1996, I knew I had to include its findings in an appendix to my book. So often the experience of ordinary people is flatly contradicted by those in authority, who often quote "extensive research" which purports to show that the accumulated experience of a culture is based on a false reality. Parents in particular, wishing to do the best for their children, modestly defer to these "experts" whose superior studies seem to have shown them more of the truth. The over-view presented here of all the research in the field of the modest chastisement of children, serves to assure people that they have no need to feel this.

The Family Research Council (FRC) is a Washington-based organisation that evaluates research carried out by different institutions in the United States. They discover who commissioned the research and why; what results were wanted from the research, and what questions were asked of participants. From this, they are able to judge how trustworthy each piece of research is. In October 1996, they published the report summarised here, called *Spare the Rod?* which was a meticulous evaluation of the various studies into the subject of parental chastisement of children. All their findings are carefully footnoted, and interested parents can access the entire report on www.frc.org.

I believe it is very important that parents and commentators are able to see for themselves how far properly conducted research programmes confirm traditional parental wisdom, rather than the passing fashions of academia. In fact, as far as I can see, there is no single detail that contradicts what tradition and experience have taught most parents. There are, however, one or two statistics that surprise because they confirm what many people might have assumed were just their own fanciful observations. Such as the fact that, above all, it is permissive mothers who have troublesome teenagers; and that women who never smack their children get angry and frustrated much more often!

One change I have made is to substitute the word "smacking" for their word, "spanking". This is purely because the debate here is centred on "smacking" which is the English language equivalent of "spanking" in American English, and it avoids making it seem something different.

To start at the beginning: the report quotes a Gallup Poll of 1995 which shows most parents citing "lack of discipline" as being the biggest problem in public education, and strongly supporting corporal punishment by parents. However, the public is often told, by the media at least, that "research" indicates that smacking is abusive and contributes to adult dysfunction. FRC therefore begins by analysing the kind of research that finds this negative association, and identifies two reasons why this is so.

Firstly, there are the studies that fail to distinguish between appropriate smacking and other forms of more abusive punishment such as kicking, punching and beating. Secondly, these studies usually include the corporal punishment of adolescents rather than just pre-school children, where smacking is more effective. The blurring of distinctions in these two areas, says the FRC, gives critics the illusion of having data which condemn all disciplinary smacking.

From this point, the FRC goes on to examine and criticise some of the unfounded arguments promoted by the opponents of smacking. FRC starts with the claim that psychological studies show that smacking is an improper form of discipline. This claim is examined and dismissed because The National Institute of Healthcare Research conducted a systematic review of the literature on corporal punishment in 1993 and found that 83% of the 132 identified articles published in clinical and psychosocial journals were simply *opinion-driven* editorials, reviews or commentaries, "devoid of new, empirical findings". Moreover, most of these studies were methodologically flawed because they grouped the impact of abuse with that of ordinary smacking. The best studies, on the contrary, demonstrated beneficial, not detrimental, effects of smacking in certain situations.

Then they examined the common assertion that "hitting" another person establishes the moral righteousness of hitting those who do something regarded as wrong. This they call the "smacking teaches hitting" argument, and it is widely used in Britain also, by self-styled childcare experts. However, there is no evidence in the medical literature that a mild spanking of a disobedient child by a loving parent teaches the child aggressive behaviour. The critical issue is how any punishment is used by the parent. In a large study of 332 families conducted by the Iowa State University in 1994, they examined the impact of corporal punishment and the quality of parental involvement on three adolescent outcomes – aggressiveness, delinquency, and psychological well-being.

They found a strong association between the quality of parenting and each of these three outcomes – but corporal punishment was not adversely related to any of them. They also discovered that childhood aggressiveness was closely linked to maternal permissiveness, allied to negative criticism. Remarkably this link was more close even than that between childhood aggression and abusive discipline.

Another often repeated mantra examined by the Council was that, since most parents smack a child in anger and frustration, this teaches the child to express these emotions violently. They found that another major study conducted by *Paediatrics* in 1995, discovered that most parents do not smack a child in anger and frustration but purposefully and with a belief in its effectiveness. In fact, the mothers who reported being angry often were not the ones who smacked their children. It found too that, in the absence of smacking, the parent was left with nagging, begging, belittling and yelling. In short, they found that smacking a child could break the escalating rage of a rebellious child and more quickly restore the relationship between parent and child.

As to the assertion that smacking a child teaches him that "might is right", the council pointed out the many occasions on which parents have a duty to use their superior power and strength to protect and restrain a child; as, for instance, when he won't accept treatment, or medicine, or when he runs into danger.

"Classic child-rearing studies" they found, had always found that some degree of power, assertion and firm control are "essential for optimal child-rearing". When exerted in the context of love and for the child's benefit, the child does not perceive it as bullying or demeaning.

Finally, this research tackles the three most common arguments used in Britain to deter parents from smacking their children. For example, the use of the word "violence" for the purpose of describing normal parental smacking is, they say, a propaganda tool, without foundation in fact. Both the dictionary definition and common parlance define "violence" as "exerting physical force so as to injure or abuse". Since there is such a clear and fundamental difference between abusive violence against a child and mild, loving, corrective smacking, no purpose is served by putting them together – except to confuse the issue.

Secondly, the idea that smacking is an ineffective disciplinary tool is also dismissed. When used in the way that most parents do, i.e. with restraint, moderation and in a loving context, it has been consistently found to reduce the subsequent frequency of non-compliance with parental wishes. Dr Diane Baumrind of the Institute for Human Development at Berkeley, California, conducted a 10-year study of families with children aged 3 to 9 years old. She found that a balanced disciplinary style, including smacking and positive encouragement, produced the most favourable outcome for the child. On the other hand, very authoritarian parents, and permissive parents who never smacked, were less successful.

Last in the litany of the psycho-babble of childcare, is the idea that smacking a child leads on to physical child abuse. In fact, the Council found there was no evidence for this at all and, empirically speaking, it is obviously not so. Up to 90% of parents smack their children when necessary and yet child abuse is way down in single figures. Furthermore, over the last ten years, reports of child abuse have increased while approval for parental smacking has declined.

Paediatrics, once again, published research on "Where Paediatricians stand on spanking", and found that more than 70% of primary-care paediatricians rejected the idea that smacking "sets the stage" for real abuse. Indeed, according to Dr Robert Lazalere, appropriate parental smacking may actually reduce child abuse since parents who are ill-equipped to control their child's behaviour, or who take a more permissive approach (refusing to use smacking), may be more prone to anger and explosive attacks on their child. He was encouraged in this view by the fact that, one year after banning smacking in Sweden, their rate of child beating became twice that of the United States. This is given yet more weight by their own government report "Statistics Sweden" which in 1995 reported a fourfold increase in child-abuse by family members between 1984 and 1994, and a sixfold increase in teenage violence.

Altogether, the council's findings are almost precisely what any parent would tell you; that in a loving, caring atmosphere, smacking a child is, at times, necessary and beneficial.

That this parental tradition, tried and tested millions of times, needs to be spelled out, researched and checked so thoroughly, is a tribute to the power of a handful of academics and media people to influence public policy in a way that runs directly counter to the experience of the mass of the population.

Common sense, as St Thomas Aquinas defined it, is the recognition of reality. You don't need to be able to analyse it – just to recognise it. Paraphrasing dear G K Chesterton again, common sense is possessed by the 95% of people who are sane; we, alas, are too often governed by the opinions of the 5% who, without it, are simply mad.

Appendix Two: Working from home

For me, one of the most surprising facts about women and work which has emerged in the last few years, is that the number of women in full-time work has not altered significantly since 1850. What has increased is the number of women in part-time jobs, of which many – if not most – are home-centred. In 1996, Dr Catherine Hakim of the London School of Economics produced a carefully researched book (*Female Heterogeneity and the Polarisation of Women's Employment*, Athlone Press, 1996) in which she dispelled many of the myths about women that are constantly repeated by the media. For example, she found that most women prefer a male boss, reject sex equality – in the sense of both sexes having exactly the same bread-winning and nurturing role – and happily depend on men for money in what they see is an inter-dependent relationship.

Her most controversial observation as far as most commentators were concerned was that there were two distinct kinds of working women: the careerist and the home-centred; and that the home-centred ones far outnumber those for whom their job is of overriding importance. Confirmation of this was provided by a survey of 2,000 mothers and pregnant women in April 2000 which found that no less than 81% of them would give up work to be with their children if they could. Only 6% of them enjoyed being in full-time work. So, far from being alone in finding the combination of a young family and work a terrible strain, today's mothers should feel able to relax. They are a majority; and the ones we hear of so often in the media, are a minority.

However, thanks in part to pressure from female "careerists", tax advantages for married men were abolished and building societies persuaded to accept dual incomes as a basis for loans – which has helped to push house prices beyond what many single-earner families can afford. In other words, the majority of home-centred women have been disadvantaged by their more affluent sisters and all in the name of an irrelevant "equality".

The number of full-time women employees has remained stable at about one third of all women for more than a hundred and fifty years, although the type of work they do is different. The big change has been in the ability of home-centred women to find part-time work to supplement the family income. Together with an increasing number of men, many women, too, are finding ways of working from home that were unknown a few years ago. Government figures show that a million people started their own businesses in the last five years and that another million are expected to do so in the next three years. Many of these will be women at home.

Women thinking of ways of making money at home are advised to start at the Job Centre, where the staff will be able to tell them about the Government's Enterprise Allowance Scheme. This scheme helps people who have been unemployed for at least eight weeks to start a small business. The survival rate is very good for such businesses and, apparently, less than ten percent of those who start out on the scheme fail within the first three years.

The reference library is another good place to go for information about the "Individual Learning Schemes" which are now operating in a number of areas and provide financial help for daytime classes and home-study courses in a variety of job-orientated schemes. There are many books available on the subject of home-centred work. The list is almost endless of things that women are now doing from home, and they range from the practical, like aromatherapy and massage, to more specialised things such as proof-reading and computer competence.

Such a variety of skills are represented by the things you can do in your own home that it did not surprise me to read, in November 1999, that American research published in *Nature* magazine had found that caring for the young triggers cognitive development in the mother. "That suggests that offspring aren't as passive as people think", the researcher said. Well, we all knew that!

Taken altogether, the potential for home-centred work is better than it has been for many years. My own two daughters and daughter-in-law live in a domestic environment that is now much more congenial than anything I encountered only twenty years ago. Above all, they know many other young women like themselves, who see domestic life as creative and fulfilling. They are immensely busy, but in a way that does not take them away from their families or their communities. Several members of my family have joined Full-Time Mothers (PO Box 186, London SW3 5RF. Find them on the web at www.fulltimemothers.org) which, as the name implies, is an organisation of home-centred women. This provides them with a useful and informative newsletter once a quarter, plus contact with like-minded mothers' groups throughout the country.

These women don't feel that they are missing anything by being at home with their children – except, perhaps, credit for doing it! In a society like ours, which does not value the housewife, it is up to housewives to make their voices heard when they can, and to band together with other women who feel the same. Their jobs can wait a few years until they have the time and interest to resume them – but their children have only one chance to grow up with the nurture and attention that only their mother can provide. Our society may not thank them for it at present, but – so what! – their children certainly will.

Index